Advance praise for *Fellow Survivors*...

In his new & selected *Fellow Survivors*, Al Maginnes is a poet summing up. Early on in this radiant collection (in the poem "Thirty Years of Teaching. No Sabbatical") we hear: "In the end / there will be a roster / of things undone, but somewhere / someone might recall an afternoon when / I said something I had not known / until I said it, a twist of thought / that became true when words found it." Allen Ginsberg, John Clellon Holmes, Charles Bukowski and others make appearances, as if the narrative of a life is nothing if not peopled by a sky of personality-stars whose work infiltrates Maginnes' great storytelling. And there is always his reaction to "the infinite stories that go on / being told for the love of their telling," as in this set of lines from "Salt, Fire, What Comes After": "...what followed / and what lay ahead, waiting for another taste / of the salt-rich blood, the tears I bore / into this world I could not vanish from or flee." The guy's a rocker. Someone I trust the way I've trusted others who earned that designation the way you earn your face: one line at a time with always one more at the margins. So many favorites in this generous, high-spirited volume, but I'd be amiss if I didn't single out "Elegy With Clifford Brown Playing Trumpet"—"the body held fast inside / the skin of the moment."

—A finalist for the Miller Williams prize, **Roy Bentley** has published ten books of poetry. His latest collection, *Beautiful Plenty*, is available from Main Street Rag.

Ravings from Al Maginnes readers from previous books:

From **George Looney** :

"Al Maginnes weaves together stories and his own brand of extended figurative tropes to construct poems that speak wisely and with the authenticity of this world in which none of us are 'fully hauned or forgiven.' These poems find beauty and solace in the idea that despite everything we can remain 'willing/ to disk burning and drowning at the same time' just to be here , experiencing this place and imagining the next, where lovemaking might offer 'one way of resolving time' and each of us can hope to be or become 'a player silent with the possibility of song.'

From **Philip Terman**:

'In collection after collection Maginnes' poetry digs deeper into his passions—for family, for com-munity, for labor, for loss and love. The poems in The Next Place demonstrate depth of understand-ing amd empathy with a breadth of reference that can intimately inhabit Shakespeare and New-town, the cosmos and 'the last dive in town.' These poems represent the best of what contempo-rary poetry can offer, and these are poems of not only a grown man, but a good man.'

Sandy Longhorn:

'These poems may zoom in on the "small matters: of daily life, but Al Maginnes asks the big ques-tions, questions of what a person leaves behind during a lifetime. In these poems of cemeteries, funeral pyres, fatherhood, and sobriety we encounter harbingers, ghosts, obituaries, and prayers. We are reminded that 'the myth says// we all get one more chance.'

Ron Rash:

'To read the poems of Al Maginnes is to encounter an acrobat of consciousness. His poems' swerves and leaps delight and amaze, but most of all they sound the depths of the human heart.'

Claudia Emerson:

'Al Maginnes situates himself in the middle of things, the poet's voice mature and contemplative, able to articulate in finely wrought poems the various ways "we are worn away by the things that shape us.' This is a wise book, beautifully rendering "in the impossible cursive of the world" both known and unknown.'

David Wojahn:

'Al Maginnes' gruff music and consummate skill with narrative recall the poetry of Cesar Pavese. He also resembles Pavese in his uncanny ability to strike that precarious balance hard-butten realism and a special empathy for those lost and forgotten lives who don't often figure in contemporary poetry. Thanks in part to Maginnes' rigorous self-appraisals and his unfussy-but-sure command of technique, these lives do not, as one poem laments, "become data." Instead they are counte-nanced and dignified because Maginnes has a heart as formidable as his talent.'

FELLOW SURVIVORS

NEW AND SELECTED POEMS

AL MAGINNES

REDHAWK
PUBLICATIONS

Redhawk Publications
The Catawba Valley Community College Press
2550 US Hwy 70 SE
Hickory NC 28602

ISBN: 978-1-952485-99-2

Library of Congress Number: 2022950839

Layout, cover design, and edited by Robert Canipe

Cover image "Untitled No.1" by Isabel Maginnes

Printed in the United States of America

redhawkpublications.com

Poems in the section titled "New Poems" were previously published in *Asheville Poetry Review, American Poetry Journal, Birmingham Poetry Review, eratio, Lake Effect, Laurel Review, Salt, Visions International, Vox Populi.*

My thanks to the editors of these journals, some of whom have supported my work for many years.

Thanks as well to the presses that published the books in which the Selected Poems portion of this book came from.

Taking Up Our Daily Tools. St. Andrews College Press, Laurinburg NC. 1997.

The Light in Our Houses Pleaides Press, Warrensburg MO. 2000.

Film History Word Tech Press. Cincinnati OH 2005

Dry Glass Blues Pudding House Publications 2007

Ghost Alphabet White Pine Press 2008

Between States Main Street Rag Press, 2010

Inventing Constellations Cherry Grove Editions, 2012.

Music From Small Towns, Jacar Press, 2014

The Next Place, Iris Press, 2017

Sleeping Through the Graveyard Shift Red Hawk Publications, 2020

The Beasts That Vanish Blue Horse Press, 2021

OTHER BOOKS BY AL MAGINNES

Outside a Tattoo Booth
Taking Up Our Daily Tools
The Light In Our Houses
Film History
Dry Glass Blues
Ghost Alphabet
Between States
Greatest Hits 1987-2010
Inventing Constellations
Music From Small Towns
The Next Place
Sleeping Through the Graveyard Shift
The Beasts That Vanish
Fellow Survivors: New and Selected Poems

TABLE OF CONTENTS

NEW POEMS

FROM TAKING UP TOOLS (1997)

FROM THE LIGHT IN OUR HOUSES (2000)

FROM FILM HISTORY (2005)

FROM DRY GRASS BLUES (2007)

FROM GHOST ALPHABET (2008)

FROM BETWEEN STATES (2010)

FROM INVENTING CONSTELLATIONS (2012)

FROM MUSIC IN SMALL TOWNS (2014)

FROM THE NEXT PLACE (2017)

FROM SLEEPING THROUGH THE GRAVEYARD SHIFT (2020)

FROM BEASTS THAT VANISH (2021)

ABOUT THE AUTHOR

NEW POEMS

(2023)

LIGHT POLLUTION

It's likely we never sleep fully.
      Science says the lights

of our devices, aglow with recharging,
      fracture the dark we need, burrow

beneath our eyes, beneath the bone-deep sleep
      bodies need. So we wake, cramped

and sore, brains already buzzing. We blame weather,
      age, bad food for our fatigue

as we reach for our phones like smokers stretching
      to swallow the first puff of the day.

There are nights I come awake in the electricity
      of 3 am, feel the junctions in my body

jangle, circuits burning, all the crossed wires
      of my skeleton and soft organs snapping

response to the glow of phone and computer,
      the passionless start of television.

Like most, I'm tethered to the surge
      and voltage of this dimension

and swim up from sleep a few times each night.
      Sometimes I get up to pee, then start

out the window where streetlights cast their glow
      and join the globe of light

that smothers all the little darknesses
      we close our eyes to hide from.

THE PARTIES THAT YEAR

It was the party where someone stabbed an icepick
        through his hand trying to dismantle a door.

I never knew his name, but someone said his father
        was a minister and owned a tire store. At each party

there was something to separate it from all the other parties.
        A china cabinet got smashed, a fire started

in the kitchen. And every weekend was a step closer
        to the day I could draw the blinds on this place, put it

behind me because I was going somewhere else. Just where
        didn't matter. I just needed to escape before it made sense

to stab myself in the hand. I remember leaving that party,
        already hearing about the next one. Somewhere, the grandchild

of that party is going on, oversized boys smashing into walls
        and each other, glass breaking. Girls beginning

to memorize some portion of the patience it takes to live
        inside this world. In the only office burning lights

on the block, the owner of the tire store reaches for
        a form, sees the star-shaped scar on the back

of his hand, a blemish he has seen so long he no longer sees it,
        forgotten as he bends to work again.

MARS BONFIRE

It's the birthday of Mars Bonfire,
owner of the best name
in rock and roll. Who but a man
named Mars Bonfire could write
"Born To Be Wild," if a song
like that can be written,
arriving as it does, full-bodied
and screaming past any
complications of birth? I don't know
where the man named Mars Bonfire
is tonight, but some part of him
should lean against a bar, shrouded
in Scotch fumes and smoke, sullen
behind the sunglasses that never
come off, creaking inside leather
he wears in public. I was too young
for parties when Steppenwolf ruled
the speakers. ZZ Top and Led Zeppelin
thundered the speakers when I was
in high school. But let
some joker drop Steppenwolf
and Three Dog Night on the turntable,
and girls started to dance,
and for two minutes and thirty seconds
we were all born for revolution
and anarchy. But no song ever played
long enough to thwart our plans
for escape. The music sped
beyond our hearing, and while
the party grew quiet, we took
another drink and planned how
it would be once we left town.

THE LIGHT OF STORIES

Every story has two halves. The teller
and the listener. Truth has no function
in rolling the story along. It needs
words that shock or collapse in laughter.
The two of you lean across a dim table
while glasses empty, speaker and listener
one now under the bartender's worn gaze.
Someone carved letters in the tired wood
your elbow rests on. The story you hear,
the ones you tell, rise from the carved letters,
the unfinished words that stare up at you.
If you had candles instead of forty-watt bulbs,
your real illumination would be a voice
trying to finish before last call.

CLOUD CURRICULUM

The sky was always my classroom, endless
unreeling of facts that required nothing more
than tilting my head and listening
for the start of the big nothing that came
before equations, the blank page
always above us,
waiting for us to translate
the erasures of cirrus, the ink spills
of storm cloud.
I've let the earth-written
books to sprawl in my lap for the hieroglyphs
of clouds and all that doesn't revolve around them.
Teachers, parents, bosses all had their turns
Explaining I'd never get anywhere
with my penchant for the sky, my knack
for tracing a narrative never quite visible,
one I detoured into during math class
or drowsing in the back seat on long car rides,
waiting for some sign from the Great Editor
of how soon this chapter might end.

One thing I believe smokers love is the exhalation,
the plume and ribbon that rises from the mouth,
lifts to the ceiling or gets
breathed in by the great lung of sky.
When a class was writing
or bent low over some quiz I would have to grade,
I stood by the classroom window to stare
at the school's scrubby grounds,
thin slice of sky over the pines and the flat
top of the library building, and I might have
been back in tenth grade math class or paused

in the wide doors of a warehouse where
work is still waitingas soon
as I finish this cup of water and turn
my eyes from an arrangement of clouds
that feather the sky, that promise,
in their don't-care-either-way manner, to
be waiting when it's time to walk home.

THIRTY YEARS OF TEACHING. NO SABBATICAL.

One of the scientists I read, in order
to understand how matter builds a universe
should conduct a study
on time's ability to erase itself
to inconvenience once the spell
of waiting is done.
                         When the gift arrives,
we forget the ordeal of waiting. I've heard
men speak of decades behind bars as casually
as I might speak of fifteen minutes.
In the out-there we don't see,
those measures, minutes and hours,
become drawn-out notes, markers
inside our expanding symphony.
                              And when
I sit on my porch, two-thirds of a life spent
in classrooms behind me, free now to write
the poems I didn't compose on the shoulders
of Scottish moors or the black sand beaches
of some nameless cay,
                         on some preserve where
half-tame birds and deer-like creatures come
to see the tracks my hand leaves crossing
the empty plain
                    of the page,
I can wonder what years add up to.

I've lost most of their names, the ones
who came every fall and spring to confront
syntax and punctuation, to let
their essays come limping forth, their shy poems
peeking from behind their legs.

                                    The past is
beyond us now. My job this morning is
the future, whatever there may be of it
while the meetings to organize the next meetings
and the papers continue to pile.
                                    But not for me.

Maybe my students believed
their tuition checks were a down payment
on the truth education used to promise. None read
the long dreams of France or Ireland I authored
while they bent over some assignment
or saw me scratch off another year
like an inmate marking his wall
with a burned match.
                          So what if
my opus on the Pigeon Creek massacre
was never written or if I never learn
Italian well enough to read Dante
in the flow of his native tongue?
So what if the language of birds eludes me?
In the end
                there will be a roster
of things undone, but somewhere
someone might recall an afternoon when
I said something I had not known
until I said it, a twist of thought
that became true when words found it.

ALLEN GINSBERG AND THE PURLOINED BIBLE

I never saw Ginsberg in person though I could have once
    had I been willing to drive three hours. The truth was
I didn't love him enough when he walked the earth, gentle,
    seemingly immortal, to drive that distance.
When I worked for Poetry in the Schools, I traveled once with
    a friend who brought a single change of clothes and the heavy
red paperback of Ginsberg's collected poems that he had carried
    out of a bookstore a few days before. We were bound
for another remote outpost of Arkansas where we would urge
    children to write in the voice of a leaf or a fish,
to imagine their bodies were planets or machines. We hadn't gone far
    before I wondered if my friend—call him Bailey—might be
visited again by the bipolar disorder he'd spoken of before.
    He'd explained that it often came after he'd swallowed
a load of mushrooms. That night, after checking into a cheap motel,
    we wandered in search of a drink, but he walked into a church
and began praying, verses composed on the edge of his tongue,
    "first thought, best thought" as Kerouac once said, ignoring
the seven years he spent writing and rewriting *On the Road*.
          On the drive home, Bailey read from the Bible he'd spirited
from our room, where I'd gotten despiritualized on orange juice
    and cheap gin, leaving me to drive the delta
    and foothills into our rocky corner of Arkansas hungover
as he alternated between Ginsberg and the Bible,
    unsure whether his soul rested in the numbered verses of the Bible
    or the automats and supermarkets, the visions
Whitman visited on Ginsberg. When we reached my house
    Bailey came in to explain opera and the construct of the universe
    to my wife but began stringing a mobile of wire, beer cans,
leaves, a couple of petrified paint tubes, all dangling from
    the light in our living room. Then he was gone into
what we had called "the great American night" in search
    of deeper enlightenment or more mushrooms, leaving his
cigarettes,
    his stolen Bible, the collected Ginsberg that Ginsberg was,
even that night, probably adding to. Before college, I worked, first

on the grounds crew and then in the mail room on
a college campus whose buildings resembled my idea of
	medieval castles. I had an hour for lunch and used it
to roam the library's stacks. Before I applied for college, I'd read
	Kerouac—even *The Town and the City*—Corso, Bukowski,
Snyder. On the nights I was able, I tried my own half-made poems,
	limping imitations that said a little about being young
and restless in the seventies, long after the Beats, it seemed, had won,
	to judge by the amount of shelf space they commanded
in libraries. When I got to college, the Beats were only referred to
	with an eyeroll meant to shred any skill or dignity
they might claim. Some years later, in my first lit class
	in grad school, John Clellon Holmes began by telling us
his best friend was Jack Kerouac and related the story
	of Kerouac coming to his house at three in the morning,
bearing the now-famous scroll manuscript of *On the Road.*
	By the time I'd picked up the Bible Bailey had left behind,
I'd hitchhiked across the country more than once, worked a score
	of bad jobs, fallen out of love with poetry and back again.
I was married, but still young, still crazed by drugs and poverty
	and the fear I might not be equal to my dreams. The future
hung like a question mark, a dull neon sign specked with flies,
	flickering like the signs in one of Ginsberg's automats.
When I found a gram of mushrooms in a cigarette cellophane
	pressed between the Bible's pages, I swallowed them
without thinking and began reading Ginsberg's early poems,
	rhymed imitations of Blake, probably written
about the time he got in trouble at Columbia for writing
	curses in the dust caked on his dorm room windows.
Later he would be expelled for letting Jack Kerouac sleep
	in his room. A few years would pass before he found
the line and language to write "Howl." But I read and fell, for
	the first time, in thrall to Ginsberg's work. When I finished
"Howl" I reached for the Bible and opened it to Revelations
	and tried to read through the maze the page was becoming.

Before long the phone exploded with news of the havoc
    Bailey was causing and my wife raged because
I had not shared the mushrooms. I was in another hotel when
    I heard that Allen Ginsberg had died. My wife and I—
a different wife—were at a conference for writers
    in Washington DC. Twenty floors below, I saw
two men yelling at each other, silent actors in a scene
    that had no clear beginning. I left them to sell
wolf tickets and watched the brief item on the news.
    Before we went downstairs for another reading,
I pulled on my t shirt with Jack Kerouac's face on it,
    thought briefly of John Clellon Holmes' book
Gone in October, the story of he and Ginsberg and Gregory Corso
    going to Lowell for Kerouac's funeral. If I'd thought of it
I might have opened the hotel room Bible and found
    the verses Bailey read to me years before or chanted
on mani padme hum until my bones relaxed.
    It seemed like something Ginsberg would have done.
But I was not Ginsberg. The universe had him now.

THE RISING PRICE OF RESURRECTION

I drove two miles more than I needed
to watch the odometer spin over
a hundred thousand miles, fresh zeros
shining up blank on my dashboard. And for
a mile I pretended I was driving
a new car before it groaned and was again
the oil guzzler, clunker I prayed would
turn over each morning. My car today
will have to make a million miles to
show me all zeros. A fresh start costs more
and takes longer than it once did, but I've
signed up to make payments until time ends
because I always believe my body
good for one more mile and then one more.

ON EITHER SIDE

My friend lists all the reasons
he's drinking again, but it's late afternoon
in the valley of my body and dark
ladders down through the branches
of the eucalyptus tree in his yard.
I know the reasons: boredom,
insomnia, weed makes him paranoid.
But mostly the tunnel, dark
and unrelenting. I know those reasons:
I recited them while I walked

to the cinder block liquor store
where I bought Jim Beam or the barstool
where desperation and hope sat
on either side of me. I know them
as well as I could once tell you
each turn on the drive to the house
where my friend lives. From
the backseat, blindfolded,
I could give you those directions.
But if the car makes one wrong turn,
if it's off by a single block,
I will never find the way back.

OLNEY

It's hard to believe you hold forth
on no stage tonight, your fedora tipped
to shield your eyes as you sing
stories of old actors, icebergs, the hard trail
a savior travels. I've seen you yowl
hard as a drunk rockabilly trio
in a joint where you check your razor
at the door. Then you opened
a stone-deep silence where
the only sound was your strings
and the half-spoken song of your voice.
I saw you perform that alchemy
a dozen times before we met
in a studio in Kentucky, before
we shared stages in Atlanta,
Lexington, Knoxville. I watched
your weekly webcast on YouTube
while your beard grew until you resembled
a 19th century novelist, a notion
I think would have pleased you. But
before I heard you play a note,
you were a character in stories
Steve Runkle told my wife about
the seventies in Nashville. Now,
your passing is legend, how
you said "I'm sorry" and went silent
onstage. I've heard too many say you died
doing what you love. Fuck that.
I want to hear you sail through
another set, and at the end call,
"Tip your bartender. See you next time,"
then sing as though there will be a next time.

LIGHT HAS TWO TASKS

Moonlight only serves for shining the edges
    of things already dark. Curved fender

of a fresh-washed car. Crown of a gravestone.
    Crescent of knife blade two boys use

to open their thumbs and press the wounds together,
    the pale scars insignia of a bond

they cannot explain or express. Tonight
    they have a bonfire to build as high

as they like, smoke chasing them
    wherever they stand before they lie

by the glowing cinder-bed and sleep
    in the glow of their new blood.

Daylight shrinks the world. Birds call.
    Somewhere a dirt bike stitches over

small hills, whining as the driver revs
    the engine to the limits of torque and gear.

The boys emerge out of night's possibility
    into flat light, linger beside

the cooling ashes though they are hungry
    and expected in their unpredictable homes.

This steady ration of flat light says
    nothing of the mystery objects carve

when the world is given to shadows, when
    what is unspoken looms the largest.

OUTLAW RESURRECTION

*Butch Cassidy's sister insisted he returned from Bolivia
and lived in Spokane, Washington until his death in 1937.*

Banks aren't what they used to be. And trains,
money-poor, move too fast to stop now. You earn
by honest work or learn the grifter's games.
Honest dollars don't stay in your pocket.
The shine of the watch chain curved
across the store keeper's moon belly winks
the dull varnish of coins, silver moons
dumped in your sack by tellers who moved

with one eye locked on the pistols leveled at them.
Hard to hold a gun on a man without
a little tremor in your hand. Now the small gun
nestled beneath his arm waits for the day
he hears a name left buried beneath the equator,
a name that means shoot or run. It wasn't
the first name he rode away from. Names,
after all, are changed as easily as a pair of boots.

A friend he died with shook his hand on a train
that stopped in New Jersey. Now he gets a box
of salt water taffy every Christmas. He gives away
the candy, never says where it came from. Being dead
teaches a man to watch his tongue. Some words—
mine, Pinkerton, horse—are no longer needed.
Evening comes. Tellers lock their drawers.
The shift whistle blows. He buys groceries

for a single man, one with few wants, beefsteak,
a cigar, a few bottles or beer or a bit of brandy
to stretch the last hours of thinning light
while it is still warm enough to sit outside
and soak up the last drops of light before
the past comes galloping like a posse,
hellbent out of the cinders of old banks,
waving headlines that were ash long ago.

THE CHARLES BUKOWSKI POLAROID

He was, you would imagine, unposed, a cigarette forked
        between stubby fingers, a drink half-done in front of him,

one more in a series of endless others on the way. He sits
        at what looks like a poolside table, not looking at the lens

but at whoever might be sharing the table, the drinking companions
        who vanish for serious boozers, leaving him

as he wanted to be seen, alone with the drink and the dark symphony
        of a poem posting up in his chest.
                                        The photo

fell from between the pages of a book I bought at a yard sale.
        On the back, someone—the man himself?—had written

his name in flowing script. By the time I got the photograph,
        Bukowski lived in Hollywood, and I was beginning to suspect

the myth of the drunken poet might have some holes in it. I gave
        the picture to a friend who loved Bukowski more than I did

at the time. She is dead now. So is Bukowski. And I hope
        that picture rests in the hands of someone who loves them both

for the bitter and lovely people they are.

MEMPHIS

For Dale Phillips

When we drove east, we had our Memphis routine. We took
an exit and found a place we didn't have to pay to park—
we were always in my gray pickup truck, last artifact
of the dream my ex and I once had of homesteading in
the rock-knuckled Arkansas hills—and walked to
The Peabody Hotel. I forget what drinks we ordered
in that spacious hotel lobby, only how expensive the air tasted,
how we modulated our voices to fit the upholstered chairs,
the heavy chandeliers above our heads. One night, just before
Christmas, a woman led three models in glittering gowns
to our table to tell us the dates we didn't have for
New Year's Eve would love to wear one of these dresses
that cost more than the two of us made in a month. After
the Peabody, where we always seemed to miss the ducks,
we'd wander to the Rendezvous for ribs and beer. Then—
there is no reason to be proud of this and no reason to be
ashamed, we were young and horny and alone—we walked
to a place euphemistically called an "adult emporium,"
in other words a porn shop where we'd exchange two dollars
for tokens. Then we'd walk past the VHS tapes, the arsenal
of unidentifiable "toys" to the doorway in the back wall
and take different directions. In rooms no larger than phone booths,
you fed a token into a slot and on a tiny screen watch
some sex act beginning or ending. Ninety seconds or two minutes
and the screen went full dark. Another token bought a rerun.
The videos all appeared to have been shot in a trailer or spare room.
In one a barely legal boy and older woman went at it
under a shelf lined with a toddler's toys. I spent the whole time
wondering where the child was. The truth is there was little exciting
about the videos. Back in my truck, we'd get coffee, light a joint
and set out to drive the length of Tennessee. Once, as we crossed
into North Carolina, snow fell slow and majestic, making the sky
larger than it already seemed. Dale talked about the book
of stories he envisioned. He'd already had a story in *The Atlantic*,

so it seemed likely he would make it happen. I only wanted
to write more poems and get better at writing them. Books seemed
far away from where I sat then. We were all appetite then,
appetite for liquor, ribs, women, money, fame, for time we would need
to do our work. Appetite for the distraction of drinks, bar talk, sex.
Ten years later, Dale's book was in the stores and I'd published
enough bad poems to make a book from the better ones.
Dale almost got famous; I never got close. It's just as well.
Out of the thousands of miles we drove, the memory
that hangs most stubbornly is one night leaving a truck stop
between two nowheres in Arkansas. As we pulled out,
my headlights waved over three dead cows in a pile
at the edge of the dirt lot where drivers parked their rigs
and left them while they went inside to buy coffee, cigarettes,
caffeine pills. I don't know how many men are needed
or what machines might move a dead cow, but someone
or a gang of someones had done it, had left a pile of flesh
to corrupt. Or perhaps they walked them out, and for reasons
of their own, shot them. Some things aren't worth knowing.

CONSIDERING BEATRICE

There is no single golden Beatrice.
It takes a long time to live a full life
and each year brings its own store of regrets
and joys. Walking four blocks offers faces
fair or less than fair for you to reject
or recall forever. By the day's end
most will have been erased to make room for
another you might consider worthy
of an epic poem. In the front porch sprawl
of final years, the old lovers come back,
unblemished as they never were in life,
but matter as much as the woman
still sleeping who never asked for a poem
but makes sandwiches just how you like them.

HEART PINE

The little fires of atoms spin fastest
at the dense center of things. Silk rosins
weave among fibers, knotting into fire
that will be the undoing of this body
a century in the growing. The smell
rises when the ax splits the log, rose
of kerosene climbing from the unsplit
heart of the tree. Wisdom says to chop it
into sticks of kindling, fire-starter
for winter to come. But there is always one
ready to toss the whole misshapen knot
into the fire, let it flame into a rain
of sparks meant to light all our coming days.

IGGY POP DIED FOR OUR SINS

Or so Sid Vicious believed when he said
he wanted to live hard and die young
like Iggy, a martyr for rock and roll.
He would not be persuaded that Iggy was
thirty by then, living in Berlin, working
with Bowie on his third or fourth comeback.
A friend who grew up in Ann Arbor lived
for a while in the trailer park where
Iggy—who was Jim in those days—grew up.
He recalled Iggy shuffling around
in torn jeans and gold lame slippers
like your grandma might wear when
her bunions hurt. I've never had
a chance to see Iggy in concert,
and Sid and the Sex Pistols came and went
so quickly they were done almost as soon
as we heard about them. My wife got
to see Iggy before we met and so have
various friends over the years; they have
their stories though Iggy never spit at them
the way Henry Rollins did at me (he missed),
and as long as Iggy and I are alive
there's hope. The fact is, Iggy was always there,
never fully in the limelight or completely
obscure. I was fifteen when
Raw Power came out. I looked for it
but never found it in stores overloaded with
the Allman Brothers and Steely Dan.
So Iggy Pop has not died and at 70 can
still go shirtless in public, a move
most men avoid after 50 or so.
I began to hate The Sex Pistols when
a neighbor who fancied himself
a devil worshipper began putting
his speakers in the window on Sunday mornings

and blasting *Never Mind the Bollocks*
at inhumane volumes. That was in the years
I claimed "Better living through chemistry"
and believed it. Young men behaving badly
need role models so we had Keith Richards,
Harry Crews, Bukowski. Iggy was already
an anachronism by then, a name
mentioned only in conjunction with
Bowie's Berlin albums. He had not died
for our sins, so we had to forge
our own paths to redemption. The romance
of the drug life evaporates and then
it's just the drug and the withering veins.
And I was never so in love with
my own demise that I planned anything
other than a long life. Eventually
the drugs slipped away and I had to grasp
that I couldn't drink as I did in my twenties.
In fact, I couldn't drink at all.
About the time I sobered up, I began
to listen to Iggy and now I heard
not a role model but a fellow survivor,
someone whose tracks I could follow
even if he walked in gold lame slippers.
Some I knew never found that path,
others hang on in bodies older than they are.
More than once my buddy Tom has said
he wonders why he was able to unwrap
the tie from around his arm, to put the cap
on the tequila bottle and walk away.
Sometimes when it's too late to blast
The Stooges or the MC5, I feel it too,
and run down that list of the missing,
aimless notes you might hear from
the band as they twiddle knobs, test

chords, pretend the audience isn't there.
Iggy always knew the audience was there.
Why else would be stage dive, smear himself
with peanut butter, roll in broken glass,
taunt bikers into beating the shit our of him?
Why else is not to bring people who hoped
he would do those very things
so they could tell stories about it later?
Sid Vicious died not long after saying
he wanted to be like Iggy. I wish
he could have been. Destruction requires
an effort, as well as someone
to monitor the wounds, to warn
how close you came this time
and tell you not to do it again. But
you always would. We had to kill Iggy Pop
so we both could walk away.

WEATHER THAT TAKES US HOME

For Sandy Longhorn

If it's true that weather sculpts landscape
then I should be writing this from a sand dune
nestled in the icy hold of a glacier.
This morning a ghosting of frost on the grass
gave way to warmth enough for shorts
and tanktops. By late afternoon, we'll be
zipped into hoodies, searching for sweaters
we shed after coffee. In the Midwest, where
you grew up, were weather vanes perched
on barns and outbuildings, and did they,
like ours, freeze with rust and point
only a single direction? In Iowa, where
I have never been, I imagine
weather being larger, more majestic, than
we can imagine or acknowledge. Where I live,
we hate to accept any power larger
than ourselves. So we die in house trailers
blown apart by tornadoes, wreck our cars
in hurricanes as we drive around looking for beer.
When I was small, we moved so often
no landscape got to mark me. Did you ever,
when you were small, watch your mother hang
wash on the line, and did you, when she was finished,
lie on the ground, under the damp sheets
and white shirts and breathe in that cleanliness
while you stared into an endlessness of sky,
one way to escape the uncertain weather
that is childhood? There is always a storm cocked
and ready on the edge of a kid's existence, a move,
a sudden illness, someone with sharp fists
ready to define the angles of your face. There is
the wreckage of a report card to bring home.
One night, not long before another move, I woke
to hear The Kingston Trio singing "The Reverend

Mr. Black" on my parents' stereo, then a woman
cursing her drunken husband, language I had
never heard one spouse use on another before,
then the dark voices of men singing the chorus
over her rage. I listened after the record stopped,
after the woman got her husband out of the chair
where he'd slept through her tirade, and I knew
the world would never shed its confusion.
I would always be driving through storms, bending
to see a little further down the road
that was, however slowly, taking me home.

DEVILS AND SNAKES

for Emily and Jamie

There are worship places, tucked deep
in the elbows of back roads, where worshippers
raise snakes as emblems of faith.
Twisting copperheads and timber rattlers
slide from one hand to another,
but it takes trust deeper than blood
to receive a serpent from the grasp
of a stranger. Things go wrong.
A snake might strike the hand of one
who's lifted a hundred of its kin.
More than one preacher, aflame
with temptation, has used his snakes
to be rid of an inconvenient spouse
or the husband of a woman he's decided
he loves. The devil, after all, dwells everywhere
and snakes are only one of his handtools.
In Sunday school, the snake was our villain,
Judas's backbone, the Snidely Whiplash
of Eden, a seductive tongue singing of
the salvations buried in flesh, in bourbon
or cocaine, paradises made to replace paradise,
pleasures grasped more readily than
eventual deliverance. A swaying girl holds
the snake's body, her being beset by grace
as she feels it twist against her prayers,
brings its face close to hers. She would die
for the snake's kiss. And because she would die,
the snake becomes her devil. The things
you would die for, those are your devils
and snakes. And they wait in coiled bodies
for you to know them and give them a name.

GOD IN RETIREMENT

The sand here is dark, stained
        by eons of tides, climates, embers

of footprints trailed by humans who,
        intent on self-immolation, find ways

to make their small prints larger
        as they race for the first apocalypse

they can find. Perhaps a shorter visit
        to the tropical universe or the one

built after this one, the one still stocked
        with breathable air, with liquors

able to give pleasure to a god.
        Still, this model survives, proof

of some self-preservation in the populace.
        A little more wine before the sisters

of the scarlet moon perform their ritual
        dance again. Still. There are mine shafts

collapsed like veins, houses burning by
        the acre. Right now a man is paying

more money for a gold chain than
        my neighbors earn in a year.

He'll wear it once or twice, toss it
        in a drawer of shiny things he'll sell

for four hundred bucks on a day when
        those few bills mean more than all the money

he let slip from him back when it came in
       too fast to bother counting.

The first shine from that trinket burns
       in the back of his eyes, climbs out of his gaze

into the storm of atoms that spark the universe
       and takes its place among the aspirations

illustrated by the sisters of the scarlet moon,
       who pour more wine, try to soothe god into sleep,

leaving us with our self-made fires to burn our wounds
       clean, to illuminate our feet as we try

again to follow the dance we will
       die trying to master.

MINDFULNESS

How many times have I missed something
my daughter or wife told me or lost
the thread of some meeting because
I was wandering an endless museum
of the imagination or was wondering the name
of an oriole at the window? When
the pitcher unwound and released the ball,
I was staring down the first base line,
my swing too late and too low.

It would be a few years before I learned
the art of observing the moment. Now
that my body is a corrupt wagon
of aches and broken parts, I might
pay attention enough to hit the ball.

That chance is gone, the way something
unsayable is lost when my daughter asks
"Did you hear what I just said?" Even
if I can repeat it to her, we know I'd gone
missing from the world that is always
here, no matter where I am.

FROM *TAKING UP OUR DAILY TOOLS*

(1997)

THE WORLD DROWNING

Black water fills our basement,
underground cousin to the rain
that has run off our roof
for three days. The basement, big enough
for my sister and me to ride bikes in,
has turned swamp, lagoon, wild place,
one thin barrier holding it
from us. Anything unlucky enough
to be on a floor or low shelf
is gone. My father is down there,
measuring the water's rise, making
an inventory of what must be taken
to the curb for the city to haul off.
At the top of the basement stairs,
I count how many steps
the water has climbed, how many
before it eases under the basement door,
an oily wave trespassing
the kitchen's slick-polished tile.
Some afternoons I watch
a TV show, three guys took a raft
down a river and wound up
in prehistory. Like them
I understand all bets are off.
The skin that covers my life
could be torn back at any time
and the same black water
would force itself into the wound.
Stacking soaked boxes on his tool bench,
my father saves what he can.
I want to step down
into the new drowning room
so that I can be baptized in its danger

until the water, furrowed by any movement,
becomes just one more darkness
like the night I once feared
closing my eyes on.
I go to sleep hearing
water that falls to rise again.

JOBS

Tools had secrets
to make jobs get done:
claw hammer, power saw
I never had the skill to use.
My hands blistered to fit
shovel, rake, and hoe handles.
When I got a carpenter's bench
for my eighth birthday, it was my father
who built a bookcase, bird houses,
a wooden key with hooks to hang real keys on.
I watched, trying to discover
the life hidden inside tools.
He tucked his lower lip under his teeth,
hammered and measures his way
inside some concentration
I could not enter, my first glimpse
of the work men invent to answer
a bidding buried in the clank
and gearwork of the daily shuffle.
It would be a few years
before I walked onto a construction job
and learned men were identified
by the jobs they were paid for.
At the finish, they left their names
on I-beams, staircases, the backs of panels.
It was there my hands hardened
with the work underneath them,
and I learned the rhythm that progresses
to the long breath at the day's end.
I scratched my name
in the wet concrete of a grade beam.
In my first office job, the progress
of paper was endless. I signed nothing

to mark the work of my softening hands.
I wanted to build something
in my unpaid hours that would hold
solid and symmetrical as a right angle,
my name the only inessential thing.
My father never signed his bird houses,
but I have seen his name scribbled
over and over in the frantic work
of a young bird's wings
as it apprentices itse;f
to the job of flight.

MY FATHER'S TATTOO

A bird of blue ink flew the inside
of my father's forearm.
Four inches higher, a patch of scar
marked a picture I never saw.
The missing tattoo may have marked him
deeper than the one that remained:
there was no story about either
told just after dark on the back porch
when the past seemed to glow
like the coals waning on the grill.

I see him in his Navy uniform
coming out of the dim parlor,
the sting in his arm forgotten
in an afternoon of beer and liberty.
He turns down the street with two friends
who will fade into cracked photographs,
a wife and family still remote
as mirrors of light
sun strikes from the ocean's rippled surface.
I used to believe the bird was real,
that it flew into my room while I slept
and my father watched.
Each night I planned to wake
and take its flight for myself.
During the years we had little to say
I stopped once outside a tattoo booth
on Carolina Beach's boardwalk
to scan the display of motorcycle wings,
mushrooms, skulls, and slogans
for my father's bird. I moved off, wondering
if I could hold in my own arm
that piece of my father,
that throbbing flight.

SALT, FIRE, WHAT COMES AFTER

It was salt I tasted when a bone-fisted boy
punched my lips into my teeth, the same
salt that Lot's wife became when she turned
to see over her shoulder the burning city
they fled. Three weeks earlier, I'd looked back
at Chicago's stained skyline and dirty snow
melting behind me, eroding like salt
as my father drove us to our new home in Georgia.
I'd seen a drawing of Lot and his daughters
fleeing into the desert, his wife behind them

frozen white by God's spare fury. I still wonder
if it was salt that she became. If the intention
was to hold her forever, why not granite?
Then we might visit her where she stands,
monument to disobedience and impulse,
the tendons in her back-turned neck beginning
to crumble a bit, eyes struck wide
from staring into that purge of flame.
Or why not sand if no trace was meant
to remain? But perhaps the desire

was for something white, easily defiled,
illustration of the imperfect soul, the fate
of weak flesh. I once walked home
backward in new snow, delighted
that my footprints would mislead
any tracker. As we moved south,
I dreamed of being made new, graceful
as fresh snow. With no past,
I might be chose for teams, be forgiven
my quick mouth and slow body. But we follow

ourselves wherever we go, our tracks
marring sooted snow and dry ground. Maybe
that's why I've always envied men and women
who disappear from their lives in mid-step,
not because of broken laws or creditors
but because some hidden limit was breached,
some flesh finally violated;
a stalled traffic light, a cashier's sneer,
and they clean out the bank account
and take a cab to the airport.

Sometimes they turn up years later,
tending bar in New Mexico, planting azaeleas
in Dalton, Georgia. They just couldn't take anymore,
they say with the puzzled smile
of one having to explain something obvious
as gravity. They refuse to return, even
for a visit. They have learned the lessons
of Lot's wife and the penalties for looking back.
The real story is never so romantic of course.
There are abandoned spouses, trashed promises,

the whole network of human grief.
We never mentioned Lot's grief in Sunday school.
Perhaps he simply refused the barter of tears
and the salt they paint across his face.
Now when I love, I seldom look back, too busy
loving the sense of flight, motion's power to save.
But two weeks after moving to Georgia, after walking
into a new classroom, my smart mouth got me punched.
The taste of my own blood swamped my mouth
as I fought back without power or passion

until someone of real size and ferocity,

tired of the show, separated us. Walking away,
flesh burning against the dry cold of a southern winter,
I wanted only to disappear. Grateful
I was leaving no tracks, I looked back
as Lot's wife had, not at the fresh start
falling in flames behind me, but at what followed
and what lay ahead, waiting for another taste
of the salt-rich blood, the tears I bore
into this world I could not vanish from or flee.

THE ANGELS OF OUR DAILY BREAD

Beside the imperfect cobble
of each task our tarnished
and clumsy hands turn to
rises the ghost of its conception,
built in imagination's pure moment
by the angels of our daily bread.
You see them in Renaissance paintings,
hanging over battles, famous births,
the claiming of new lands,
there to bless the work but helpless
to halt mistakes. See the worry
pinching their tiny eyes,
pouting their frightened lips
into empty kisses. Our realm
of bent nail and shaved door,
of the wired muffler and the slow leak
must puzzle them. In their kingdom,
doors do not stick. Clocks run.
Fountain pens hold their ink.
Flawless symphonies soar all day.
Some crafty hands seem to know that place
and bear down on every task
as if this chair or tire or sandwich
might be taken by an angel.
I once worked for a carpenter
who drove each nail, made each measurement
with such steady accuracy
that I believed some impatient angel
might have whispered to him
of a place with no clumsy helpers
or crooked boards or mistakes
in the plans. "I can make it work,"

he'd say, eyeing some tangle
my hands had made and gather himself
around the task, an angel's incense breath
cooling the back of his neck.
I flexed chapped hands and watch
the job move one step closer
to the shadowless creation
that the dream given us
each time we take up our daily tools.

SHARKS IN KANSAS

"Florida," she said. "Paleontology." That afternoon,
May flattening into summer's long humid rows
might have remained where I buried it,

had I not read this morning
that the fossilized remains of a shark's jawbone,
fifteen million years old, were uncovered

in a Kansas riverbluff. I've heard that the weight
of air will crush the organs of sharks brought to land,
drown them in their own airless blood.

We cannot relax, become dangling bait
in the weightless element that sustains them.
Yet there are times gravity weighs down

our bodies as well. For two years, she
and I tracked each other's moves,
both of us in love with other people

and happy most days, but curious
about the quick flame of sun
on water we had seen in each other.

The single time we touched, she passed me a pen
and dry static ticked. Our hands flew apart,
afraid of being shocked, afraid of a time

electricity might not stop us. And tonight
I can imagine her taking my fleeing hand, saying
"Touch here," pressing my palm flat in the warm

dirt. "They used to swim down there,"
and, for a second, I'd swear I felt
one of those old hungry bodies, appetite
keener than instinct, passing below us

so deep we'd feel no ripple
until, half a continent beyond my imagination

of our bodies, the shark, mouth filled with food
and blood, turns at the water's plankton-rich edge
to find the sea a dry shelf behind him and dive.

There are sharks, sharks in Kansas, still
swimming in water that has turned to stone,
bent in the memory of tides

to the exact angle I once saw her arm bend
across her lover's shoulder, the way
my wife out her arm around me

just as the theater darkened last night,
the way small boys hold to each other
before they become afraid of what touch can mean.

Maybe that fear never leaves us.
When she said "Florida. Paleontology,"
I did not move to wrap her in the thoughtless hug

I might have offered someone else, but said
"Arkansas" and "poetry." When she asked, "So when
will I see you again?" we both knew the answer.

We would remain finely separated
as bones in a skeleton, bound
but differing in every form and particular.

And if there was regret in our bone-thin smiles,
at least there was no blood on our lips
as we gave each other to the sweet
quiet afternoons of what might have been

and plunged into the currents that would bear
our cruising appetites afloat as we kept moving
to hold the land-bound weight
of our bodies from crushing us.

FAIRY RINGS

Neither the wedding waltz
of dust-starred mites
nor the buck and wing
of cloven hoof dances
the brown rings into the grass,
but the teenage mother dangles
those bedtime enchantments
before the sleepy child
to keep him from the scarier truth:
the slow grind of fungus
that chews to wet stink and splinter
the tree stumps buried
by landscape and back fill,
the hidden use earth has
for what is trusted to its care.
Now the rot works up
as tree roots once worked down
and the old tales are dusted off
for dancing one round more
in flimsy shawls of leaf mold and wind,
for who among us would not wake
in the dankest, crumble-hearted
night hour to witness
the fairies' circling ballet, blessing
from a world so close to our own
we find the tracks its tenants make
leaving a mother's mouth,
the one place
science and magic lie together.

FROM *THE LIGHT IN OUR HOUSES*

(2000)

THE MARRIAGE OF CLOTHES

There is a story, whose truth I don't know,
of a man who escaped from a chain gang
and changed his prison fatigues for a pair
of overalls hung on a farmer's clothesline.
The next morning the farmer found his pants gone
and dressed himself in the dew-wet prison clothes
that lay there and went to work. Before noon,
a posse discovered him splitting wood
behind his house and hauled him to prison
to finish the sentence of the man who stole
his overalls. When his time was done,
he walked home in the prison clothes that got him
arrested in the first place. His wife was gone,
the house a yawn of empty rooms, the fields
a long neglect of brambles and weeds.
The farmer walked out back and found his axe
still lying where it fell when the posse
grabbed him. He set a slab of wood on the block,
found the old habit of chopping once more.

If it ended there, the story would wrap
into some neatly folded Zen parable
about suffering and acceptance. But
this story, like most stories, does not
happen alone. The escaped prisoner
kept going until he came to a town
where he exchanged the farmer's overalls
for a factory worker's clothes. In these,
he traveled to a city where he stole
a banker's suit from a laundry truck.
Decently dressed, he found a position
in a dry goods store where he marked time
among bolts of patterned cloth, shoes made to fit

no human foot, jars of dusty candy,
and coffee beans, dreaming of the suits
he would buy the afternoon he got paid.
And when a woman with the silence
of great distances about her walked in—
the woman most readers guess right away
is the wife of the farmer doing the time
that belongs to the man behind the counter—
he unravels bright tongues of cloth for her,
untangles snarls of ribbon, preamble
to their inevitable marriage of clothes.
The wedding night undressing, desired
and undelivered as the farmer's final axe blow,
lets the story continue, ignorant of
or ignoring our need for conclusions,
the gaudy clothes we wrap narratives in,
wearable emblems of our finite selves
and the infinite stories that go on
being told for the love of their telling.

PUNISHMENT

When William Byrd arrived
at his lodgings and found
the door locked, his servant gone to bed,
he recorded in his journal
that he woke the man and beat him.
Byrd neglected his prayers that night
but noted that he enjoyed
"good health, good humor &
good thoughts, thank God almighty."

Almost three centuries later, my student slams
her hand like a joyous gavel
on her book, declares any man
who beats his servants unfit to read.
Each generation sees all that came before
reduced, the way things seen
through the wrong end of a telescope
shrink beyond our view. When my father told me
that he and my mother did not sleep together
until their wedding night, my laughter
must have struck him like a fist.

How do we defend old sins
except to say it was done that way
then? I wince when I recall
my response to my father, a kind man
attempting what guidance he could.
For years I could not give
my family's dinner table talk a rest
as I put the whip to war,
racism, poverty, all the evils I considered
my parents the sleeping disciples of.

One day I will be lifted
from my own long drowse to learn

the banality of all my good intentions.
And when the blow falls on my back,
punishment for being a lazy servant,
won't it feel good to be the one
lifting the last, convinced
of the justice in each blow?

THE CHALLENGE

Not my first trip down that road diving
and twisting off the blacktop. But this was night,
so I couldn't see the thundercloud of dust
our tires broiled. One of these tarpaper-sided houses
was where my mother picked up and dropped off Lee Ann
who twice a week cleaned our house and watched my sister and me.
Tonight my father drove. In the front seat stretched a silence
longer than the new miles between our house and hers.

On the back seat beside me rested a box of toys
my parents had decided my sister and I no longer needed.
When I rode here in the daytime, I leaned
into the front seat to watch Lee Ann's chickens,
dirty feather clouds, cluck and scatter. One day
the summer before, her neighbor stood from chopping weeds
to mop silver sweat-gleam from his face,
and I asked *How do black people get to be black?*

They're born that way. My mother hushed me
more quickly than Lee Ann shut her front door,
offering no glimpse of her life down here.
When my mother tried the next day to explain the difference
between races, I was simply relieved to learn
I couldn't turn black the way Mr. Bryan had teased I would
if I spent any more time in the sun.
My father stopped the car in front of Lee Ann's house.

We'd never parked before. Usually the pale dust
of our arrival barely settled, falling motes whirling
in dense sun, before the car made its pivot
and churned out again. But my father picked up
the box of toys, followed Lee Ann across
her moon-washed yard. I walked silent in their wake.
Few details of that room I'd stretched to see into
return now. The man and two women

in the front room went silent at our entrance,
their talk strained to polite, uneasy smiles.
Then the children, two girls and a boy my age,
appeared from the back hall, rubbing their eyes,
clinging to the sleep dark they, half-dressed,
had walked out of. Their eyes fumbled
from the box on the floor to me and back.
I could have tried to initiate them

into the best use of each toy, showed them
how to repair the airplane's wings when it fell off,
to substitute pennies for missing game pieces.
But facing each other across a quiet deeper than child-shyness,
our silence carved one more chapter
into our inherited history of silence.
The boy finally spoke, answering Lee Ann's attempts
to coax a thank you. *I can whip you*, he said

so quietly it had to be true. When my father laughed,
the other man dared a dawn-slow smile. Lee Ann's son, encouraged,
slapped the air until his mother's single warning
froze him. This was Alabama in 1963,
still no place for anyone black, no matter
how young, to challenge anyone white.
When we left, my father's headlights cast
all that lay before us in bold, white relief,

the rest dropping into shadows too thick
to see the end of. I have traveled some distance
from that place, yet in the child-time that knows
only present tense, I will always be there, the challenge
I cannot answer still in front of me.
And his raised hand, palm-flesh so close to mine in shade,
still maps the shared condition sun cannot bleach or burn away,
this thing we still have not thrown away or outgrown.

ELEGY WITH CLIFFORD BROWN PLAYING TRUMPET

After Larry Levis

In the mystery I'm reading, Clifford Brown
may or may not have left behind more music,
something worth speculating for those who love

as I do how the quick angles of his playing
sound new light on a tune's surface

the way sun finds new faces
in the quick-peaking roofs of waves.

For the last month I've been reading the elegies
Larry Levis left behind, searching through them
as if the words, the bone-white space

between words, harbored his death. Somewhere
in those laments for seasons, for ancient horses,
for a world that is filled, not emptied, by loss,

lurked the hand that will come one day to touch us,
perhaps when we are right in the middle of things,

& lead us into a puzzle of streets
that we only understand slowly we will not
find our way out of, although that matters

less & less as the blacktop buckles & thins
to cobblestones, then dirt, as we walk out of our shoes
until we are walking on nothing & then

we are not walking at all & the way back
to all we have left undone is forgotten.

One person has already died in this novel
& others probably will, falling in the unremarkable ways

characters die in fiction—to further some plot need
or because they have outlived whatever use
the author invented for them. Larry Levis once said

that when his first book was published he waited
for a year to become famous & did not write for a year,
a necessary silence he outlasted.

More than once, in the throat of some dark arena,
riding the frenzied pulse of a rock and roll band,
I made myself believe that somehow

we would, player & listener, outlast silence,
the moment's fever suspended & stretched
drum-head tight, the body held fast inside

the skin of the moment. But the band always stopped.
House lights came up like a dirty imitation sun
across a quiet so deep & sudden it seemed like deafness,

the audience one-minded & numb, shuffling to the exits
leaving behind blankets, wine bottles, every brand of litter.

And there were always two teenaged girls
from a town three hours away, abandoned by their rides,
& one could not stop crying long enough to say her name.

Walking our new dog this afternoon, I watched her chase
the ink-black birds that gather on the sun-painted hill
behind my house. They scattered in quick scattered flight,

notes from one of God's unspoken solos.
I watched the dog chase first the birds, then their absence

reminiscent of how we chase the dead, trying at last
to pin them down, as if their lack of motion

might halt our confusion. As day has burned
to its cold end, as my hand has chased
the quick-flying birds of my intention down the page,

I've been listening to the recordings of the Max Roach-
Clifford Brown bands of the fifties. I'm going to listen
to the tunes Clifford Brown recorded the night before

the car crash that killed him, then silence,
the place every note of music, every word,

even this one, finally falls down to.

THE LANGUAGE OF BIRDS

What does the river say to a woman
sleeping beneath a window left open
so she can hear its murmur and roll all night?
With first light, migrations of birds
will rise out of damp tatters of grass
to fill the empty tent sky raises over water.

The birds do not know the river's name,
do not spend hours, as she does, watching
its topography. They only know the blood-urge
lifting them into flight, the compass guiding them
down the wide alley of water. And the woman
sleeping below them is filled

with the language of birds,
her limbs weaving patterns of flight
as if she might rise at any moment
from the ropy nest of sheets, as if this house,
the car that ferries her to a job
she endures, the little square of garden

she turns anew each spring,
mattock blade lifting like a wing
to bury itself in damp soil,
all could be erased if the next motion
might discover her in flight.
Once or twice a week, after work, she drives

to a bar to drink and watch day smolder,
bed of burning feathers, the deep, temporary red
a glaring screen across the window. Sometimes she takes home
a man with the air of other places about him.
In bed, most of them are quick and clumsy,
as if they do not trust her not to vanish.

In the morning, the river looks wider,
less passable than before, each of them
shuffling through farewells rehearsed
since their bodies rolled apart. Still,
she dreams of the one whose hand
will awaken upon her, will translate flight

into the world of flesh that is also
the world of disappointment. Only in sleep
does she progress toward the invisible
places birds and rivers know.
Once at dawn, she startled a gray water bird
out of the high weeds whiskering the bank.

Its wings wide as any man's span,
it rose with the slow assurance
of one who carries his destination
wherever he goes, who knows
that any resting place is temporary,
no matter what name is given.

FROM *FILM HISTORY*

(2005)

BEFORE ELECTRICITY

Evenings then were music, saw-grass rasp
of fiddle, thumb and horn-tipped fingers

frailing a reedy banjo, or the spinning forth
of words unspooled like thread to repair

the simple fabric lives were clothed by.
But once the lightning-born genie

of Franklin's kite came bottled and lay coiled
within walls like a snake, the world grew past

one row of trees picket-lining a field's edge
or the distant purple crown of a hill.

Conversations bustled past the death-bloated deer
on the road's margin, glimmer of new perch or bass

in root-lined ponds, to strike mothy flight
for distant and mostly invisible arenas of light.

Few mentioned how this hard new vision carved
faces and bodies, but more than one might have yearned

for the forgiveness smeary oil-light granted,
a glow built as much from shadow as illumination,

when a wife shed the day's tired dress and reached
to let stiff hair fall. And before the room was

given wholly to dark, her husband might see
the mute instrument in the corner,

its rust-scaled strings as silent as the two of them
lying in darkness that could dissolve too easily

to be trusted with any sound they might make.

FILM HISTORY

So I find you again, Dr. Stevens,
not in a classroom's closed universe
but in the tinhorn piano that scored
the silent movie I watched last night,
echo of you providing "Blood and Sand"

or "The Gold Rush" with a live soundtrack
on the classroom piano. I find you
tucked in the titles of films you mentioned
in class, saying one film leads to another
while their names filled my notebook's margins.

Entering your dusty basement domain,
the only classroom in the building with a
a piano, we were barely aware
film could claim a history. Sitting among
desks and furniture stored and unwanted,

we watched the same ninety seconds
of film run until we breathed every nuance
of its making. When you stepped in the cone
of grainy light the projector scooped
from the room's semi-dark and pointed to

some unfelt presence we had missed, the scene
kept unreeling in the wrinkles and folds
of your shirt. Too much of what you said has gone
like commands cornermen bark at fighters
between rounds or the instructions teachers call

into the push of students leaving class,
but the scene from the film always spooled forth
the same way, and the day your body became
your enemy, showed us the depths of
our inadequacy has not changed either.

The bow-tied grad student still threads the film.
The two girls in front of ask each other
what you have just said. The fitful lights buzz

and dim as they have since our first day of class.
And you fall from the middle of your sentence

to the floor and land with a sound I heard once
when a side of beef smacked a concrete slab.
We see what has happened. None of us moves.
Does the air grow too thick for us to breathe?
Like a fighter hearing eight, you stand

in the newly-charged room. No one sees the screen
your hand waves at. This is drama beyond
the refinements of plot. Here is conflict:
the boxer ordered to dive, the drifter
enticed into murder by the boss's wife.

You fall again. This time we help you up,
Fetch water, loosen your tie. Medics, grim
as townspeople in a black and white Western
who watch the outlaws arrive, wheel you out
of the room. With a tongue that has forsaken

language, still you want to speak. You will return
to finish the term, but never again
will the air spark as it did in those moments
of our helplessness. Never again will
movies—now they are only movies again—

be more than shadows pretending life
and their stories—students who inspire
a professor hard with failure,
the delinquents redeemed by knowledge—
will only be ciphers, figures eclipsed

by the vision we saved of one who felt
the universe tilt but who rose before
our screen-blank faces to fall again
alone with his single instinct to stand,
to stand and tell us what we did not know.

FOR A GLASS OF RED WINE

I want to reach over and move you
so your smoky odor of crushed grape
        cannot drift around me, but
I cannot stop watching the smear
        of candlelight reflected on your ruby belly,
bright as the hourglass marking
        the black widow I killed in my tool shed
this summer. Once I loved
        your mystery uncoiling on my tongue,
the dark and gleaming veins you opened there.
        And I loved your earthy cousin, beer,
who bears the brassy accent of wheatfields,
        and your sullen friends bourbon, scotch, and rum
who might end the party singing
        sad Irish songs or smashing furniture
and beating the host. But what
        I loved, finally, was the blackness you brought,
the stars dying one by one. I kissed you good-bye
        long ago. Still, when I see mouths purse
with meeting you, see the dim coal
        of an eye suddenly waken, I recall
your first kindliness, blood-glow
        I could believe for the length of your burning,
rapture I could ride until pre-dawn woke
        fear of what forgotten hours held.
But if I could believe your first singing moments
        once more, diamonds flaring against velvet
to deny the dust stones become,
        I'd grab you from where you sit
and swallow, pouring one emptiness
        into another until we are two
hollow bells ringing to be filled
        and filled again until the swirl commences

once more, swirl of voices and light
    of blood, tiny cyclone
in the clear barrel of a syringe, swirl now
    of my wine-colored blood in tubes taken
to be tested or measured, to tell me
    how far this new disease has marched,
how far this medicine might push back
    the death I see resting there
as surely as I see it squatting
    in the black bore of every bottle, every tilted
glass of wine. "Kill it," Keith Greenway urged,
    passing me the last bird-sip of bourbon
he'd hoarded by small doses from
    his father's bottles, the first time
I surrendered to the gentle rocking
    held there. I was fourteen.
"You could have been killed," I'd hear
    for the next seventeen years, after
the car wrecks, bar fights, nights in jail,
    nights passed out in corners
or empty lots, all the baggage
    a good drunk knows is part of the trip.
But now, I know that for many of those years
    of passing out and waking up, my death
dwelled inside me: the unknown years
    my liver smoldered, shriveling
around this disease I just learned the name of,
    that's led me to a regimen of pills
and injections more strict than any
    I've ever answered, even more strict
than the stone-thick craving for you
    I still carry. The slow burning
of my liver might stall or even reverse,
    but one scent of your dry breath
can make me thirst again
    for the cup after cup I emptied,
searching, I thought, for the pearls
    some kings used to hide in wine

for favorites of the court to find,
        round and drowning
and, briefly, the color of blood.

THE DIGNITY OF USHERS

Their authority did not unfold
from ironed white shirts and thin ties
or from the funereal seriousness that struck
their acne-splashed faces but because
they stood heir to our native faith in light.

So we followed the thin white wave
of beams they pointed down aisles
to seats we never thought of refusing.
It was the first job I wanted,
especially after birthday outings

far from home showed me the glowing
outfits worn by big-city ushers, their get-ups
a blend of doorman and military dictator,
as gaudy and fine as the plots
of movies my Saturdays were swallowed by.

None of us knew, as they took us
into the artificial light of cinemas,
that they walked the path of the pin setter,
the blacksmith or elevator operator,
professions reduced to curiosity

by wandering time. Only in the quick steps
of floor salesmen, the slim backs of hostesses
bringing us to our tables, do they remain
the artful flutters of their flashlights lost
in dark we are left to find our won way through.

LATE WORDS FOR THE MOON

There you are, old moon, old rock-in-the-sky,
still holding when I rise on shaky legs
for water to wash the bitter powder
of the sleeping pill from my tongue. How have I come
so untethered from your pull I must be unchained
to the time-release anchor of these capsules?
Tonight, all I have failed to do seems important.
You, first marker of man's aspiration
to heaven should understand that. Tonight,
the slow disease that percolates in my liver strips
too much of the world to the bones sleeping
beneath each silken veil. Centuries of poets
have sung to you, dressed you in the faces
of their beloveds. My house is dark, and you
and I are face to face, my blood becoming syrup,
the pitted lozenge of your face a chart
of where I have not been. Let me look at you
without forgetting how the pill dissolves in water.
Let me find the right notes to make hymns
to speculation and desire. I know men have mapped
your surface, given names to your valleys
and dusty ridges. I know the right machines would
let me stand on your surface like a street corner
the way I'm standing here, one hand tight on this glass,
the other clutching the counter's edge. Let me be grateful
for the slow work of these pills. Let me come to you
another light with something like longing.
I know better than to believe you are listening.
But I have to say this, and there you are.

SPIRITS

Though it's been over thirty years
since I sipped any drink stronger
than coffee or non-alcoholic beer,
I still have a pulse of the old ecstasy
when I pass through the portals
of a bar. And while I believed neither
the turtle-backed Baptists of my youth
who called whiskey the devil's work
nor the inspired drunk who proclaimed
alcohol God's gift to man,
the mid-afternoon dim of a bar,
the slow upwinging of smoke
create a stirring in the soul, one reason
the ancients called them spirits.
It dreams for us. Lift a glass
and see what cloudy essence swirls there,
the unnamed name of what sings
deep within the choir of bottles.
And if the body cooks itself
above that blue flame, is twisted
in the shape of a tired bar rag,
we must know the pleasure continues
beyond pleasure. The first time
I went to the altar to let
wine become blood, I could not
suspect the opposite to be true,
that flesh could unravel
into alcohol, smoke, careless words
that drift ceaseless as prayer
from our bodies, vessels able
to be filled or emptied by spirits.

THE BLUES AND THE ABSTRACT TRUTH

The Hawks meet Sonny Boy Williamson,

Helena, Arkansas

Later they would tell of their shock
upon discovering he spit
in that can not tobacco juice
but blood. But they could say nothing
back to the deputy sheriff
who ran them out of town
for eating in a black-owned joint
on the dirt-road side of Helena.

One short afternoon of playing
blues in a rented room, sipping
home-made liquor called Blind Tiger,
stood no chance of knocking over
measures more strict than the twelve bars
they'd swapped around all afternoon,
these five white boys called The Hawks
and one dying black man who looked

sharp in his London-tailored suit
strutting Helena's dusty streets.
Sonny Boy would soon be dead
and The Hawks would be on the road
with Bob Dylan, that afternoon
the slurred harp-notes history plays.
Then Dylan would fall from his bike,
and they would become The Band.

That afternoon, Sonny Boy told them
about his trip to London, about
the English boys whose names would soon
be on albums stashed in bedrooms
all over America. "They want
to play blues so bad, and they play
so bad." Last time I saw The Band,
Richard Manuel, soon to die, sang

"I Shall Be Released," his face burned
white in the spotlight, spectral,
as alone as Sonny Boy, dead
alone in a borrowed bed, as alone
as the deputy who brought law
written nowhere but in the dust
of Helena's streets, in the blood
of men and women who walked there

through customs framed by decades
of power's silent arrangements.
This was what they had come to see,
what Sonny Boy couldn't tell them
when he spit blood in a coffee can,
then blew for all he was worth,
screaming out riffs until time would let them
practice until they could play.

TOWNES VAN ZANDT (1944-1997)

"all born to grow and grown to die"

—*"Rex's Blues"*

It seems fitting to have forgotten
the first time I heard his voice
since so many of his songs resurrected
the swamp-dark of pre-language

we've built civilizations to deny.
He spoke of writing "Mr. Mudd and Mr. Mudd"
in such a frenzy it seemed his hand might fall off.
Other times he imagined having

no hands at all might cure the soul-deep
terror that carved long caverns through him.
Our oldest music lies buried
in such night-blankness, bone rattling bone,

clawed fingers drumming stretched hide,
sound whose ferment helps us forget
our short wait for death. The first time
I saw him play, a man spoke from the front row,

saying they'd lived on the same street as boys,
biography we didn't expect of someone
so thoroughly built of wind and ash,
his face a collage of hollow bone and slant rhyme.

"Is that you, Bill?" Townes did not quite smile
as he squinted down a valley mapped
with broken strings, uncapped pints, nightmares
written on envelopes. He shook hands, then,

delicate as a spider dances, finger-picked "Colorado Girl."
If you hear his thirty years of records, time pulled
his voice deeper and slower, distilled it
with regret, with vodka and cigarettes and sleep

that brings awake a thirst that is fire
joining fire. And the songs change.
A rambunctious boast—"Guess I'll keep a rambling/
Lots of booze and lots of gambling"—becomes

clear-eyed self elegy for a man
who would bet on whether
the numbers on the gas pump ended up
odd or even. "Daddy's having a fight

with his heart," was how his daughter reported
the last struggle of his life. Six months before that,
I watched him, shaky with living and booze,
which were, by then, the same things

as he hacked away at his guitar, losing his way
through words many of us knew like breathing.
No one spoke or stopped watching. Finally, silently,
he stepped into the off-stage dark, giving

the club to the cave-deep quiet
you can hear on some of his last recordings
when the stretch for a note or word
echoes the fight to control

the first instrument, the struggling heart.

"WHERE LATE THE SWEET BIRD"

in memoriam, Tommy Flanagan

Birds loop and spin outside the stone gates
      of winter's fortress, descending
only to pick stubborn ground, never completely
      disappearing from this place where winter
is mostly improvised and the week that finds
      bird tracks scrawled in snow is followed
by the week of muddy thaw.
                   In here,
      Sunset and the Mockingbird, the concert
recorded on your sixty seventh birthday changes
      the season cast over our downstairs rooms,
and as much as I might wish to claim
      some forewarning of your now-arrived absence
from those tunes, each song refuses
      to give up the bone-rattling life
your attention granted them.

§

      So who will sing for you, old elegy-maker?
Who will play for you as you played
      for Ella, Monk, Coltrane, Thad Jones,
spirits already flown,
              spirits
I might once have claimed waited to add
      your harmony to their passing names,
but it seems clear now that we are
      brief passages, bound only by the framing
artifice of music, of speech and geography,
      the invented ways of tying
one life to another,
             of denying
the silence each note falls to.

§

We have descended to the short days,
their light a spark grudged from flint
          the air a cousin to stone,
                              when the gathering chill
demands from us the deliberation
          I saw from you at Memorial Hall
the single time I saw you play, your dry patter
          between songs leaving us unsure
whether to laugh or not. And somewhere
          in the second set, as the bass player bent
further into his already too-long solo,
          you shared a quick shrug and a grin
with Kenny Burrell, the two of you waiting
          for the cascade of deep notes to end
so you could get to work.

§

On the job sites and in the warehouses,
a radio was always hammering
          against the bicker over which station
to play.
          A hand was always reaching
to take the music from soul
          to heavy metal and back.
                              The Detroit car factories
were no place for music but the workers brought
          their swollen hands and tired backs, their ears,
pounded nearly deaf by steel on steel,
                              to leave behind their jobs
while you did yours,

         nodding in time to the quiet craft
learned during a thousand nights
    at the long-flown Bluebird where you learned
to follow melody down the most-tangled path.

§

This is weather we earn
    our passage through, when even the warmest music
becomes a fist of seeds scattered
    across dry and stony ground. This is not
elegy, only one more map of a season
    when you become a flurry of notes waiting
to rise from hands wiser than mine,
    to shade the horizon long enough
to gather our attention and briefly enough
    to be named beautiful
even though such quick disappearing wants
    the body's songs to fly with it.

TRANSLATING THE DOGWOOD

Who can negotiate the shadow-web
cast by the calm dogwood
that did not blaze but whispered
its way into full blossom?
Soon I'll walk outside to drink in
how gently the season has turned in,
sneaking in like the guilty husband who,
shoes in hand, eases open the back door,
tip-toes the creaking stairs. Yet,
each year one more of the dogwood's limbs
dies into bone, no longer dreaming
the green fire of new buds. In the story
my friend told of her mother's moving
out on her father, each day they carried
one or two pieces of furniture away,
arranging what remained
around each new absence until
the emptiness was too great to deny.
But by then they were gone. It was spring
and although they were broke,
her mother planted flowers until
their yard was a banked fire
of color. The world tells stories
we should do our level best to listen to,
but the slow-growing riot outside lets me
believe that whatever this earth has
to tell is written best in the calligraphy
of shadow the twice-damned dogwood lets
fall over soft grass, in the lisp of wind
humming under soft leaves, in this dirt
we stand rooted in, no matter
how we aspire to blossom or flame.

FROM *DRY GLASS BLUES*

(2007)

DRY GLASS BLUES—ONE VERSION

"From a lyrical point of view, the art of 'writing' blues songs consists of combining phrases, lines and verses with compatible emotional resonances into associational clusters that reflect the singer's own experiences, feeling, and moods with those of his listeners. And more often than not, the result is truly original."

—Robert Palmer, *Deep Blues*

This sunset, swaddling the undersides of clouds
a pale red, reminds me briefly, guiltily, of an ale
that was the only beer on tap at one bar I went to
in my years of strenuous drinking, a drink that
I liked so well I kept ordering draft there even
after they switched to a dark beer that sat heavy
and ponderous in the glass, swallowing the light
that set the red ale gleaming, a glow I imagine
across the face of a guitar I never saw
or heard played but whose description I heard
so often I would know it today if I saw it
hanging in a pawn shop window or slung over
the shoulder of some picker, the gleaming finish
darkening from gold at its center to blood shade
of midnight red at the edges. This is the light
of final things, the dull, dusty fire that falls
over a job site just before the order to
gather up the tools, when the first inch-thin breeze
of the day touches salt-baked skin. In this hour
bars prepare for the after-work drinkers, the ones
who hurry to outrace their thirst. I remember
all of this, but know that one part of memory
is invention, so the truth hides somewhere between
this telling and the next. The risk of such telling
is that stories learn to erase their complications,
to run more smoothly to the desired end,
until memory is trusted as a kind of truth,
like Caleb telling me about nights of jamming
with Jorma Kaukonen or John Hammond Jr.

or how he slipped into one of Clapton's sessions
and watched Clapton unloose a twenty minute blues tirade
that left the other players sweating to keep up
but went unrecorded in LA's best studio,
like the cloud-thick heat of a summer evening,
Caleb playing the guitar I let him borrow,
scattering notes and riffs like there was nothing else
for him to do. "Play 'Dry Glass Blues,'" Delores said
and Caleb frowning. "Let me see if I remember it."
His thumb thwacked the brass-gleaming E string, he fingered
a pair of jangly notes and stopped, flexed his fingers,
tried again. This time he found the path of the song,
thumb striking the strong bass, index and middle fingers
skipping the thin line of melody. "Dry glass blues,"
he mumbled, the only time I would hear him sing.
"Dry glass blues/ Throw up my hands/ Say
What's the use/ Ain't gonna lose/ Those dry glass blues."

This was in the summer of my first recovery
or my first try at recovery, after the wife left,
after I understood that my life had dwindled
to three or four bars and getting home, although
covering the two blocks that housed those bars could take
most of the waking hours in any one day.
I made the slim armatures of a living
teaching two sections of freshman comp a semester
while I completed or tried to complete
the manuscript of poems that would be my thesis.
I'd used the student loan to pay my rent ahead,
planning to have a summer for writing. By the first
of June, I'd written nothing and had not been
to bed sober in nearly as long. That was how I came
to the AA meeting in the basement of the VA hospital
one Sunday night. I'd been to one meeting when I was married
and knew if I got there early, someone would want

to introduce himself, to talk and hear the story
I was still too much a part of to tell. And I wanted
to shake no one's hand until my hands could stop
shaking on their own. So I arrived precisely at eight,
poured a cup of coffee and took a seat by the door.
The discussion part of the meeting had just begun
when a couple walked in. The man, taller than me
and knife-thin, his curly gray hair past his shoulders,
his jeans a maze of patches, got them each some coffee
and took the chair next to mine while she doctored hers
with sugar and powdered cream. His half-smile could have been
recognition or simply feigned surprise that two men
such as ourselves could end up in such circumstances.
If he recognized me from one of the nights when
memory had failed me, those nights that always took me
by surprise, no matter how often they occurred
I wanted to hear nothing of what I had done
in those blank hours that faded like film
I saw melting in a projector once. One second
the actress was onscreen and saying her lines,
then she dissolved in a smear of flame-orange,
drowning in the white rectangle of empty glowing
light on the screen. I would be drinking, and then
I would be waking, at home if I was lucky
but sometimes in alleys, a patch of trees, a porch,
great black chunks of time vanished, and I had no need
to hear what unforgivable thing I had done
on any of those nights. Already my life seemed filled with those,
some of them complete strangers, who seemed to feel honor-bound
to catalogue every stupid thing I'd done when
they'd seen me drunk. I fixed my eyes forward,
he moved his chair to make room for the wide-hipped woman
who dropped a hand glimmering with rings on his knee.
When the meeting ended, I made for the door before
anyone could introduce themselves or say

they'd seen me before, either in a bar, or last year
at the meeting I'd gone to wearing a wedding ring.

The next day I didn't drink and found a meeting,
this one in the basement of a church. I got there
just before eight, parked the pickup I had managed
to keep during the divorce by promising to make
the payments on it (I thought that my divorce
must be the first one ever to have a clause in it
concerning the custody of dogs, but a friend
who worked as a paralegal told me he'd seen
people squabble over fish, paintings, mixing bowls—
anything to discomfit the companion turned other).
The couple from the VA meeting walked by me
on the way in, and he nodded. I knew it was
unusual to see couples at meetings. In a few years
my second wife and I would attend together;
it would, for a time, be our version of a date
on Saturday night, but I was two years and hundreds
of drinks from meeting her. Since then I've seen members,
usually men, bring wives or girlfriends to see them
pick up a chip. Usually she would sit as still
as she could, face wrinkled with fear or disapproval,
but mostly drunks attend meetings alone. The two of them
were whispering when I walked in, but he pointed
to a nearby chair and offered his hand as I sat.
His name was Caleb, she was Delores. I introduced myself.
After the meeting, Caleb asked, "You want to get
some coffee, man?" They had no car, so I drove
to an all-night diner where everyone seemed
to know them, and we drank coffee until I was
too wired to sleep once I got back to the house
grown increasingly empty since my wife left,
not only because she returned now and then
to grab a lamp, a chair, whatever she needed

to make her new place more comfortable, but because
it seemed fitting that summer to live with bare floors
and empty walls I could bounce off of.
                                                    The next night
I gave Caleb and Delores a ride to a meeting
and our pattern was set—a ride to the meeting
coffee and a ride home. Bits of our lives began
to leak out—Caleb had been a musician
but worked as a carpenter now. Delores came
from New Orleans and had been a "dancer"—never
saying what kind of dancing she had done, but the name
of that city and the word "dancing" would always
remind me of being fifteen and walking
Bourbon Street for the first time, my friend and I spying
through the open door of a bar a woman dancing
naked or close enough to naked for two
virginal and aching boys, that shadowy glimpse all
we would have to sustain us a while longer, and even
when it happened, none of the shy girls we would know
would fling themselves with such abandon as that
faceless woman sliding against the bar's humid,
velvet air. We looked until the bouncer asked, "Well?
You boys coming in or not?" and we hurried away,
wishing we had gone in and stared until our eyes filled,
but how could I remember that sight more clearly than I do?

"Dry glass blues, dry glass blues/
Gonna walk a hole in these shoes/
Just to fill those dry glass blues."

It was heroin, Caleb said, that killed his music career.
Heroin and bad timing. We were in their trailer
on the south end of town where rent was cheap, car lots
advertised good rates on weekly payments and bars
offered lots of easy trouble. Caleb and Delores

confined their trouble to arguments with neighbors,
problems paying bills and hiding from the landlord.
When Caleb told me this, I'd just gotten some coffee
and a slice of Delores's dry cake. Off of booze,
cocaine and crystal meth, she filled empty hours
cooking, girdling her waist and hips with pounds she tried
hiding under the too-large clothes she wore. Even if
few strangers would pay now to see her naked,
Caleb could not keep his hands off of her, combing
his long fingers through her hair, tracing the curve
of her shoulder with a hand that might seem disinterested
if his attention were no so constant.
Sonny Terry and Brownie McGee were on the stereo,
easily the most expensive thing he owned.
I remember almost every bit of music
Caleb played for me and recall as well how he treated
those records—all of them fairly new—like museum pieces,
holding them only by the edges, lowering
the tone arm as precisely as a surgeon makes
the first cut. He rarely turned the volume up high,
but his speakers, waist-high and heavy, remnants
of the seventies ethos of bigger being better,
rumbled the floor. Caleb shook his head when I asked
if he still played. "Don't even have a guitar anymore."
He put on Miles Davis's *Kind of Blue*, music I thought
I knew the first time I heard it. I'd known Caleb
and Delores for three weeks, the longest I'd been
without a drink since my second year of high school.
Behind my eyes the tiny goblin that wanted
more than coffee and stale cake capered and chewed.
That night I had been called on to share at a meeting
and had been appalled to hear myself mouthing
the flattest clichés of recovery—"Let go
and let God," "One day at a time," "Easy does it"—
aphorisms either Zen-like in their warm mystery or stunning

in their stupid plainness, phrases I had mouthed
as precisely and emptily as a parrot
might say them, "superficial yet profound" as one reviewer
said of *Leaves of Grass*, which I was reading again,
trying to feel again the spark it had the fall I started college,
when I lay on my bed reading and felt I was being levitated.
"No, man," said Caleb, "I haven't picked a guitar
up in what?" He looked at Delores. "A year, babe?"
"Not since the night before we stopped drinking," she said,
scooping one more thin slice of cake onto her plate.
I knew there was more to the story than I was hearing
about why they left New Orleans and came to this town
where the first knuckles of the Ozarks crowned the hills,
a place, the local joke goes, that will be islands
once the polar icecap melts. I wondered about
my notebooks of poems and whether or not I would
keep writing if I really gave up the booze,
a question that ignored the fact that I had written nothing
for weeks or months before I started going to meetings.
I ignored that fact so well that on the way home
I turned down the street that housed all my favorite bars.

A time arrives when memory creates itself
and I might be telescoping the night of
Caleb's revelation about no longer playing
into the night I parked in front of Roger's, distorting,
in other words, the facts of the story but not
its truth, and I may not have given much thought
to writing at all. It was simply a truism
shared by almost all the apprentice writers I knew
that writers had to drink. And a time would come when
I would stop drinking and not write for a few months.
But not every story can be told at once.
One day during the next two weeks I wandered
into a used record store and bought two tapes by

Lightning Hopkins because Caleb had said Lightning was
one of his favorite players. Then I went to Roger's.
When I found my way back to the meeting
in the basement of the VA, after a Sunday-long hangover,
Caleb and Delores were there, smoking cigarettes,
weak cups of coffee cooling in their hands.
"Hey, stranger." Caleb shook my hand. Delores's brief hug
was an unholy wash of tobacco, perfume and chocolate.
"We wanted to call you," she said. I had no phone, a lack
that quarantined me from AA's preferred means
of communication. One potential sponsor had turned me down
because I was phoneless, telling me that without daily phone calls
there was no point in trying to work together.
Caleb and Delores did not ask where I'd been,
but when I told Caleb about buying the Lightning Hopkins tapes,
he slapped my knee. "You might be learning something," he said.
At their trailer that night, Caleb put on Sonny Rollins
and told me to listen. He started the story
of Sonny's two year exile, practicing under
the Brooklyn Bridge, but segued somehow into
the story of his band leaving Austin for L.A.,
intending, as he put it, "to sell out and make it big."
It was the mid-seventies, heyday of The Eagles
and all the slick-sweet southern California bands.
"We were better than them," Caleb said, thin fingers
twisting as if they meant to rebuild music out of
cigarette smoke, coffee steam, whatever could be
reshaped to the purpose of memory. Gigs came,
first opening in clubs, then headlining.
There were some brief tours and the shiny warm-up jackets
favored by record label reps began glowing
from their audience. "We were so full of shit,"
Caleb said. "We wanted them to make us rich
and kiss our asses while they did it." Delores knew
this story and had gone to sort laundry or fold clothes,

the quiet, undemanding tasks there are always too many of
when more than one person lives anywhere.
When the band finally signed a deal, it fell apart.
The producer heard a record different than
the one they were making. Fights broke out, tracks got erased.
And there were problems besides the music. By now
Caleb and two others in the band had discovered
heroin, embracing it like converts to a dying cause.
By the time the band played its last gig, Caleb showed
only because he needed money to score.
The album was never finished. What there was went
into the company's vaults, the musical
equivalent of purgatory. I wondered
if he still had a tape of the band around.
Caleb looked embarrassed a moment, then said
he might have something somewhere. He would look.
In the silence that came after this part of the story,
he found another record and put it on.
I knew this one—Willis Alan Ramsey's one album.
Years before I'd had a winter-long fling with a woman
who had only four or five tapes in her car, and this album
had been one of them. The rest of the story was
predictable—an attempt to get back together,
a final splintering. A new band, this one comprised
entirely of junkies. Then the attempts
to kick, weekends trembling and puking only to run out
and score on Sunday night, equipment pawned and sold,
a stint in rehab, then another, a few clean months,
and relapse. Finally he left L.A., drove dope-sick to Austin
and kept going until he reached New Orleans
where he got high again. Soon he met Delores
and the two of them fed one another's habits
for a while until they decided to get clean.
"And here we are," he said, as though it were that simple.
It's never that simple. Caleb had gone to work for a contractor

he met in the bar where Delores danced. One night
they went to a party at the contractor's house.
Caleb bought his Martin, the only guitar he had left
except for the red Gretsch he had owned since he was sixteen.
After midnight, things turned ugly. Neither he nor Delores
could ever remember why three strangers pushed Caleb
outside and punched and kicked him until he could not rise,
only watch as their venom turned on his guitar,
their boots stomping through its polished face,
snapping its neck. Caleb leaned forward to show me
the thin scar under one eye, the bent nose that would
always point back to that night if he ever got
too close to forgetting it. No more, he decided
the next morning. No more booze. No more dope. The surprise was
that Delores would go along with him, They came home
from their first meeting to find their door kicked in,
Caleb's red Gretsch gone. Was it then that I offered
the use of the guitar I'd owned for years, a gift
from my ex-wife? I'd never learned to play well enough
not to bore myself, and I warned Caleb not to expect
too much as we drove to my house. Caleb tuned
the guitar and patted the dogs pushing close
and curious around him and Delores.
I shut the dogs in a bedroom just as Caleb pulled
a slow riff I would not have believed possible
from that guitar. He grinned as he began
to work his way down the neck and back up,
Delores inventoried the tier of dishes
rising out of the sink, the book and papers stacked
so randomly it was impossible to say
where clutter stopped and squalor began. "You need
a woman to take care of you," she said, but before
I could answer, Caleb hit a loud chord. Delores gave
the guitar the same look I'd seen crossing the face
of a woman who saw another woman

kissing her husband at a party. Anger, fear,
competitiveness ran liquid across her face
before she composed her stoic mask. Here was
the thing that could take him away quicker than booze
or dope, this simple box of metal and wood.
Caleb, his ear bent to an out-of-tune string, saw
nothing of this.

"Dry glass blues, dry glass blues/
My woman says I got to choose
Ain't no jelly can fill/ those dry glass blues."

        When I dropped them at their trailer,
Caleb told me to wait, went inside and came out
with a handful of records. "Give these a listen.
Let me know what you think," he said. I flipped through them.
Willie Dixon. *Sketches of Spain*. Mississippi John Hurt.
Monk's Greatest Hits. Leadbelly—names and titles
I'd heard of but never had the chance to listen to.
Now, I hardly go a week without listening to
Sketches of Spain but it sounded too much like
classical music to me when I played it that night.
But when I heard Mississippi John Hurt play
"My Creole Belle," I listened to it half-a dozen times
in a row, wordlessly joyed by that simple blend
of dry voice and fingerpicked guitar. When it rained
a day or so later, I drove to their trailer
knowing Caleb would not be working. I found him
talking on the phone they'd gotten the week before.
He hung up and poured me the coffee they liked,
a dark-tasting, chicory-flavored blend. They kept a pot
brewing all day. "Know where I can buy a pistol?"
he asked, handing me the cup. I shook my head, surprised.
We lived in one of the easiest states to buy
firearms in. The year before I had taken

a friend, a woman whose old boyfriend would not hear
the "no" she kept giving him, to look at guns in a pawnshop.
We were both drunk, and she talked the pawnbroker
into taking a check, which must violate every rule
passed down among pawnbrokers since the first interest
was calculated on the first item offered
as collateral on a loan. I could remember
the questions she had to give answers to but little else.
Caleb picked up my guitar, strummed a slow chord.
"Things might be changing soon," he told me. "We could
be coming into some money." He picked up some notes
and stopped to check his left hand. "I'll have calluses
again soon."
                    A few more days passed without drinking
I turned again to my thesis. One afternoon
Caleb and Delores did not answer their phone,
But when I got home, they were in my front yard,
waiting to show me the truck they had just bought.
The body looked like it had been beaten with one
of Caleb's hammers, but the engine growled low and smooth.
They might be heading south for a visit soon,
said Caleb, and they were tired of taking the bus.
Delores spoke sharply for the first time in my hearing;
the bus had been good enough to bring them there.
I could sense something hanging off-balance, seething
between them. Caleb gave me a half-grin,
a wry wink intended to say *women* and asked
if I wanted to go for a ride. We wound up
on the mountain that looked over town, gazing down
from the parking lot of a church that had erected
a giant blue cross that glowed over the town
like the never-ending judgment. More than one
sinner, it was said, had changed his ways after looking
up on the hill and seeing that cross shining there.
Sun dropped a day-ending haze, a honey shade that set glowing

the houses and buildings we gazed down on, muted
brightness that struck promise from all it touched
and the three of us sat, perhaps mulling what promises
we had yet to fulfill, silent as worshippers.
Delores leaned her head on Caleb's shoulder
and kept it there until he started the truck.
Halfway down the hill, Caleb told me he thought he knew
where he could buy a pistol and Delores flared.
"You don't need no gun," she snapped. "You need to start using
your head." Caleb yelled that if he thought he needed
a gun, then he by God needed a gun. Their argument
carried us through a red light, and I'm not sure
they noticed when I got out at the next stop sign
to walk home, the futile echo of their voices chasing me.

*"Dry glass blues/ Done laid me down/
Been chasing my thirsty/ All over town."*

I had not wanted to admit how much I had come
to depend on Caleb and Delores but in the solitude
of my summer, they had become my closest friends.
The next night or the night after, Delores appeared
at my house. I let her in, her oily perfume
a musk rekindling fantasies I had allowed myself--
Caleb mysteriously absent, Delores and I caught
in a room that seemed all bed. But she was not here for that.
She curled on the end of my couch and began
telling me how worried she was about Caleb.
They were supposed to have some money on the way,
but he was spending it like it was already here.
I knew how Caleb and Delores courted crisis, how
some disaster was always being averted
just as another one took shape on the horizon.
My life must have seemed safe and privileged to them
because I was in college with the leisure to read books

and not work. Delores shifted on the couch,
both of us too aware of the way her black skirt,
an outfit I'd never seen her in, rode up her thighs,
how light shifted when she moved her thick legs.
An ankle bracelet gleamed on one leg. When we had been silent
a beat too long, she stood and I walked her to the door,
half-pleased we had not betrayed Caleb or one another,
half-despairing that I would never see what hundreds
of drunken frat boys and businessmen in New Orleans had seen.
That night she arrived in a dream so real
that I woke up, convinced she was there. In the dream,
she had been onstage, shrouded in a thick white nightgown
but tossing pasties and garter belts to the crowd,
then turning from me to show everyone else
what was hidden underneath her gown. I woke up
sweating and got a drink of water. I opened a book
and read the rest of the night, then slept all day.
I woke up and went to a meeting where I thought of nothing
but frosted mugs of beer and how Swifty used to have
my beer opened and waiting before I reached the bar.
I came home white-knuckle sober and grim to find
a note from Delores in the door. Caleb had come
home just long enough to grab some money and take
the truck. Could I come get her so we could look for him?
I recalled her raw perfume, thought of her alone
in their trailer a few miles away and went
by myself to look for Caleb. I found him in Roger's,
where I still owed a few dollars on my last tab.
"Professor," said Caleb. "Buy you a belly wash?"
He lifted the beer bottle in front of him. I got a Coke
from the machine and listened while Caleb talked about
the gold-top Les Paul he had just been to look at—
"a real guitar, not like that crate you loaned me"—and might
buy when his money got here. I finished my Coke
and waved to Bird, the night bartender. He gave me

a beer. Here is what drinkers do: they drink.
And they argue with drinking. So when Caleb and I laughed
about how pissed off the people we knew from meetings
would be to see us drinking, it was laughter with a hook in it
tearing our throats as we saluted our failure.
I've forgotten the end of that night,
only that I woke up at home with my truck still parked
in front of Roger's. I walked downtown to get my truck
and six hours later called a cab to take me home.
The next night I sipped cheap whiskey and listened
to Leadbelly sing about death and faithless lovers.
The night after that, I picked up my third white chip
of the summer. Delores and Caleb were not
at the meeting. Afterward I drove to their trailer,
found it locked and dark. I went home, made coffee,
read *The Confessions of Nat Turner* until the sky began
to sweat the humid gray of summer dawn.

"Dry glass blues/ Be bound to end/
Bottom of the bottle/ Everyone my friend/
Wake in the mornin'/ Cryin' again
From the dry glass blues."

The next day I went up to the English department;
school would be starting soon. Some friends were back
and I went with a group of them for a beer. I left
after two and drove home congratulating myself
for proving I could drink moderately when
I needed to. I made a pot of spaghetti
and washed dishes, telling myself that this was
a new start. To prove it, I opened *The Sun Also Rises*,
a book I'd failed to get through at least three times before,
and read until the late news when I put the book
face down (where it stayed for months) and stretched on the couch
to watch stories about school board elections,

a nursing home being shut down. When I saw
a sharp profile I knew but could not place
flashing on the screen, I sat up just as the ticker tape
voice of the news announcer said that a couple wanted
in connection with a bank robbery in Texas
had been arrested here in town. The camera bobbed,
then I saw Delores lifting her shackled hands
to cover her face. A bank guard had been shot
and paralyzed in that robbery, the reporter said.
I waited for more, but the news went to commercial.

"Dry glass blues/ Burn my mouth/
Dry glass blues/ I'm headed south."

Maybe it ends there.
                          I never saw Caleb
or Delores again, but the story, at least this version,
goes on for a while yet. A few nights later, leaning
on the bar at Roger's, I recalled my guitar.
I put a six pack to go on my tab and drove
to their dark trailer. The front door was unlocked,
and my guitar was leaned against the wall, untouched
in the chaos of the overturned room. I strummed
a few chords. Whatever music Caleb had spun
from that guitar had gone with him. After I put
the guitar in the truck, I went back inside. There was
beer in the icebox. I did not think of it as stealing
when I began carrying Caleb's records to my truck.
When I'd loaded all the records, I took another beer,
made a half-assed attempt at wiping my fingerprints
from the surfaces I'd touched. Beside the stereo—
I wasn't drunk enough to take the stereo; that would be
too much like stealing—I found a tape with my name on it.
I stuck it in my pocket and drove home. The one story
in the paper said Caleb and Delores were caught

because they called the partner who'd been with them
for the last robbery. He needed to get out of some trouble
and when Caleb called him, he let the FBI know.
If I have not told this story too many times,
I remember it well enough to invent ways
of getting the stalled machinery rolling, of finding
detours around the parts that don't exactly fit.
My thesis was accepted the next spring. I left
town, quit drinking finally, married again and more or less
found my way into this life that has become,
for better or worse, my own. Each of the last few
phrases deserves many more sentences, and will get them,
but not here. It is nearly sixteen years since I saw
Caleb and Delores. I read somewhere that bodies shed
enough cells that we are made new every seven years.
So I have become a new man twice since the last time
I saw them, and they, wherever they are, have been renewed
as well, metamorphosis that happens so slowly
there is no time to be aware of it. I should
try to close some circle here by saying I still
listen to the records I stole from Caleb
or even that I think he would approve of my theft,
but they went a few at a time, sold for beer money
or swapped for records I wanted more, the ones
that remained finally banished when I switched to CDs.
Caleb and Delores are probably done with
the prison time that I assume waited for them
in Texas, and they may be together again,
Caleb banging at songs from his days of glory
on Sunset Strip, Delores baking fudge, remembering
how sunset seemed, for a moment, to bathe
the Quarter in dusty fire that has become,
for her, the color of memory. It was a while
before I listened to the tape of Caleb's band—
first I lost it and didn't find it until I moved,

then for a while, I had no tape deck. When,
at last, I did listen to it, it held no significance
beyond the casual pull of being curious.
I didn't care much for what I heard—string-sweetened
country rock, songs about leaving and good women
and whiskey, the same thing a hundred other bands
had done just as well. I listened once and put the tape
among the others I don't listen to but don't
throw away. As I live longer without drinking,
the years I did drink become ever more distant
and more ominous. I was lucky finally
to stop when I needed to stop, so the days filled
with the grim back and forth of that summer remain
part of my memory of that summer. As time changes,
memory does as well, and now my clearest image
of Caleb and Delores is of the red Gretsch,
a guitar I never saw, the one stolen while
they were at their first AA meeting, the loss
that pushed them to carry out the bank robbery
they had always joked about. Memory could not be
any clearer than this:
                              Delores drives
into the bank parking lot. It is summer and dry air bakes,
heat rolling thick as steam off of the black asphalt.
Caleb tells her again what to do while their accomplice,
who, in this imagining, looks too much like me for comfort,
checks his gun once more and the two men leave the car,
caps pulled low, sunglasses covering their eyes,
shirttails hanging loose to cover the handles of their pistols.
Delores waits in the barely breathable air—
this, and not the scene in the bank, is always what I imagine—
her watch ticking off the three minutes she was told
to wait until starting the car. She turns the key,
hears two dry and precise gunshots. She is pulling
out of the lot when Caleb and his partner come running.

The next morning, after the car is hidden, the money
split, Caleb and Delores take a bus north to Arkansas.
Where we would meet. Where things would hover a while,
then fall apart. I'd been sober for a decade
when I read a book about the LA music scene
in the 60s and 70s, and there, two-thirds through the book,
was the name of Caleb's band, an outfit, the writer said,
"noted for incendiary live shows" but whose "single effort
at recording in the studio was aborted when
Caleb Waters, the band's lead guitarist, and Si Magee,
the drummer, took the master tapes—at gunpoint,
according to some sources--and dropped then in
the Pacific Ocean." Wondering why I'd never heard
that story, I found the tape and played it again
but turned it off for the memory of Caleb picking
"Dry Glass Blues," a song I have never uncovered
in years of flipping through bins of used CDs
and vinyl records, of asking collectors until
I have come to believe it was a song invented
just long enough for me to hear it—was it only once?—
and keep through all the changes of memory and flesh.

FROM *GHOST ALPHABET*

(2008)

GHOST ALPHABET

Enough letters have fallen from
the theater's marquee to make
the feature's title unreadable.
The patrons will be little help:
some are walked from a group home
for the handicapped or bused in
from the assisted living facility
or they are teenagers stoned on X.
They are there because tickets are cheap,
because light and sound occupy them,
not because anyone cares about
the story unraveling on the screen.
The white space shining between
the remaining letters is pages unwritten
titles and plots of films never made.
Monk said the notes not played
matter as much as the ones that are.
So the invented or guessed at titles
write themselves in a ghost alphabet,
words structured over the frame
of whatever letters remain.
The couple on the aisle, sharing
a bag of rubbery popcorn, don't
remember that they were not married
to one another. Content with dark,
they won't notice if a reel repeats
or plays out of sequence
as sometimes happens. As long
as there is sound and motion, there is
a story to be made from it.
When letters were too plain a task,
the monks assigned to copy documents
began embellishing their script
with drawings, animals curved
in the shapes of letters, seraphim

blessing the wide margins until
decoration began to overwhelm
the precise geometries of text
just as improvisation might
swallow melody. However imperfect
their showings, the movies always
begin on time, relieving
any audience there is of having
to make stories from the wide blank
that echoes the space between letters
and all that finds itself written there.

FIREFLY GOSPEL

Because we have made them the intermediaries
        of the stars and, by extension, the planets,

we endow them with an existence larger
        than the glimmer of one night

or one season, their summer bloom and flicker
        one constant of our time-fogged span.

We know or believe we know how brief
        a firefly's span, since they die

so easily once captured, but the fire hovering
        green-gold and planetary

in the emptiness between trees might be
        the same glow that cast its lamps

over a back yard in Alabama forty years ago,
        glow I ran through the dark to capture.

Each morning the bodies were shriveled and smelled
        of dead copper, but the hot, burning dimes

of stars always surfaced and were echoed by
        the weaving ballet of fireflies, more light

than anyone could capture. Now I have learned
        those lights, like human voices, are signals,

go-betweens for bodies tired of being told
        they will die, a beckoning

to the oldest orbit bodies know, but I see them
           exactly as I have always wished to see them,

small, stark missionaries descended
           to deliver night's gospel of fire.

LEGEND

Because I know her name from
rock and roll biographies
and the legendary death
of her first husband, because
I grew up hearing her voice
on my father's folk records,
because I love the myths
that accompany music
almost as much as I love
music, I should have gone
to see her when she was booked
into the coffeehouse run
by a church whose articles
of faith have been held secret
from all but the devout,
because, better than teachers
and classmates, I remember
those times a line from a song
chilled or awakened me from
the seemingly endless sleep
that is childhood, and she,
as much as any, could claim
some of those moments. But
I did not want to hear her if
it meant I would have to be
proselytized by shiny-
faced acolytes of the brand
of salvation peddled there
with coffee and cookies,
and why would she be singing
in such a place if she was not
a walker on that secret path.
Still, my whole family sang
her songs, those quick instances
of harmony rising from

the record's dusty grooves
to claim a place in the myth
of my family as well
as in the rock and roll myths
I once memorized
the way others learn scripture.
Like most who went to hear her,
I would have only been there
to gaze briefly on the altar
of her past, not to hear her
new songs or her new faith
Faith is what we have left
once we survive, even though
we owe our past the kindness
of a visit now and then.
Time might have
warmed and deepened her voice
that could once reach high enough
to freeze bone at its marrow,
but I didn't go and now
whenever I read or hear
her name I'll know she was
right down the street, singing songs
I don't remember not knowing,
Even if all she had done
was chant the famous names
of her dead husband or her
new god, even if she denied
completely or insisted
upon being defined by
her past, even if time has
done to her what it has done
to all of us, I should have gone.

ARRANGING THE POETRY COLLECTION

Begin with some mysterious lines,
                              designed
to pull the reader forward, the way the eye might
work to capture the drunken wandering
of a butterfly. Next, establish knowledge:
                              the dates
of battles, obscure coronations, the location

of The Psychedelic Furs' first rehearsal.
                              The sequence
comparing the father to a clock should come
in the book's valley,
                    where the decision is made
to finish or abandon altogether. Next, a bit of irony will
show you have a sense of humor and don't

take all of this too seriously.
                              End in rapture, whether
it grows out of lyric depths or the pills you rattle
in your palm each morning.
                    Make sure
the title can be taken at least two ways
and that the author's photo makes you slim and wise.

TO THE ONE WHO STOLE MY LAWNMOWER

I know who you are, just as you knew
        which pane of glass to break to unlock
the window that let you in my tool shed
        so you could walk out with my lawnmower.
The toolbox, with its quarter-century assortment
        of hand tools, was an afterthought, thrown in
to sweeten the pot for whoever bought
        the mower, handing you enough for
a couple of rocks, perhaps an hour
        of the smokable high you would be prowling
to feed within moments, my broken window,
        my lawnmower and tools hardly enough
to break stride for. I know or think I know
        what failures lie in back of you, what classrooms
closed their doors, what minor indignities have
        ambushed your entire life, and I know, I know
I should be more forgiving, large enough
        not to be angered at the loss of mere possessions,
but the wink of broken glass beside the road
        reminds me I almost sliced my foot
on glass from my own window.
        Prompted to recall, I peer again
through the hole that once held glass
        and see blank floor where my mower stood.
I try to practice forgiveness, but I admit
        that when I borrow a neighbor's lawnmower
or stop some chore to run to Lowe's
        to replace one more tool I used to own,
I happily devise tortures for you
        that would shame the hardiest
of horseblood-drinking Mongols.
        Fire is often involved, and rodents.
The twenty ounce hammer you stole
        and a box of common nails. But I have
tortures for myself as well: imagining

my lawnmower in rusty pieces or stalled
in high weeds, splattered by soft mulberries
            and bird shit while my Estwing hammer
and power drill lie abandoned on some job site
            or consigned to a heap of tools in the trunk
of a car, rubble that accumulates until
            each piece loses its first function.
Like anger. Or instruments of torture.
            Oh, I will spit venom at your name
for a while to come, but the truth is
            the loss of my lawnmower has become a story
and, like most stories, gets told for laughs.
            But I can laugh even when, like today,
I sweat like a rented mule, forcing
            the motorless contraption I use to cut grass now
through high weeds, because my life is not yours.
            That is what I could not forgive.

THESE ACCIDENTS

We've taken a wrong turn somewhere
and now we are two couples in one car,
late to a Christmas party, navigating
a neighborhood where lane blends
into lane, where houses pose
on well-scaped yards, placed precisely
as bells of confectioner's sugar
on a cake. One of us is reading
the useless directions, another
willing her cell phone to work
while the driver asks again,
"Weren't we just here?" and then
we are all laughing into
the valley of our helplessness,
which opens, as all things have
and will, as byproduct of
the largest accident of all,
the shotgun blast of exploding matter
that became the universe, its billions
of bits of debris spread
like pollen to take any root
it could find, any form
that could be managed, accident
upon accident, strands of being
woven and rewoven to become
the single end we are brought to,
realm where people are placed
as randomly as stars, and, like stars,
joined in formations only named
after finding their arrangements.
Nothing stirs on this street
whose name might as well be the name
of the last street; no cars move,
no doors swing open or sigh shut,
there is nothing to betray

the expensive serenity
of this community, where
our friends had to ask permission
to build a dog pen, where
the only visible motion is
the vine-pulse of holiday lights,
each house a well-designed outpost
of cheer, its display engineered
to demonstrate a sober balance
between exuberance and good taste,
the icy light of each façade
making it a bit more difficult
to dream what anger or passions
once lived or might live still
inside the blind wall of curtains.
Even now a furious hand
might tip the shaking wine bottle
a splash too long or pull back
the shade to see who passes.
A teenager is breathing through
the hours until the house falls
into sleep, and she can
slip out the back door, into
the schemes and manipulations
these streets were designed
to be a quiet haven from.
No matter how far we drive,
how lost we get, we carry
the map of insufferable humanity,
the will to survive no matter
the cost. So it was when
three mythical kings crossed
a cold desert, guided by

the arm of an angel pointing them
toward a star, and so it is
now as we, guided by no star,
no part of heaven,
only the scribbled code of street names,
white stare of headlights
casting their glaze over signs
that say nothing of the direction
we should travel, we four
still not certain if we have
grown up, who have come this far
embracing the misdirection that has
all our lives come like solar wind
to take us to towns and jobs
we never conceived in the snugs
of childhood. Those particles,
fragments of solar debris,
had to land somewhere, had to bind
to one another till they gained
a form and found a language
and creed they could share, a way
to give names to all that lay
around them, a way to rescue
what they saw from the distant
and anonymous gravities
we are spun out of, white
and faceless as snow. If snow came now
to cover these streets named for
movie stars and British royalty,
we could stop bickering about
whether King Arthur crosses Chaplin
or Fairbanks intersects Queen Mary,
but no snow is forecast. The sky remains
empty but for the cold fire
of stars, distant as the ember

of candle flame that glows
a moment in the body
of the wick after the flame
is snuffed, determined to hang on.
The knack for survival
that commands us to turn
to one another, to seize hands
and refuse against all reason
to let go, must be the instinct
allowing us laughter
as we follow swept curbs past
thin pines and boxwood hedges,
the skeletons of nameless trees.
Then a street name someone thinks
she recognizes, a turn, and we are
coming to our destination
from the wrong direction
the way we have arrived
at so many things, things
we aren't thinking about now
as we climb from the car
and hurry to the celebration,
breath rising from our bodies
like ribbons on small gifts
we open and forget, already
reaching for the next one.

FROM *BETWEEN STATES*

(2010)

ERRORS THAT MULTIPLY INTO CATASTROPHE

No bats. No prong-toothed wolves
      or rapacious coyotes. No menace
firm enough for a bullet
      or dram of mundane poison.
It might be simple weather, the storm
      television has tracked for two days,
storm with the name of a woman,
      that flickers my blood till I wake
and walk a shadow thin
      as a second hand over dark
kitchen linoleum. The storm might turn,
      descend on us like a hawk
that whispers blood and drops
      onto a field mouse weaving
its skittish path through long grass.
      In a news story before the weather,
a man I've known for three years,
      his face glazed with the pinched look
of prey, proclaimed himself
      innocent of the charges of fraud
against him. Last week he was
      a local success; now he is
a character in a story with no safe neding.
      Lately I read mysteries
so quickly I forget their titles,
      not to fantasize revenge
or justice, but to dwell a while
      in that elemental world,
where logic, however moody,
      governs action and decides guilt.
The characters who survive
      reach the end with their faith intact.
If the storm comes, it will come
      too quickly for love or faith,
will leave innocent and guilty alike,

the torn-loose wires and helpless
shards of lives struck and scattered.
        Storms gather, like a book's chapters,
in the realm beyond guilt
        and innocence. Perhaps I read so much
because I want to erase the pages
        of errors that multiply
into catastrophe, friends
        who become defendants. I want
to believe the thin explanations
        for bounced checks, payments missed,
work contracted and never done.
        I want to sleep and wake to find
the storm passed, saving us
        the trouble of speaking her name.

A BROADCAST FROM FLYOVER COUNTRY

My pocket transistor, the size of the packs of cigarettes
        I was just starting to smoke and hide, same as the one
                my father took to games so he could keep up
        with other scores while he watched the game
in front of him, could pull in stations from across the map
        after midnight, if I stayed awake that long. Before then,
                there was only the local station and one
        from two towns over that only played big band music
and Paul Harvey. Our station spun the national anthem
        at twelve, then went off the air for fifteen minutes before
                a preacher came on to testify and sing hymns
        in a broken acapella. The airwaves were his until
he was exhausted. But he always waited for the studio to clear
        the last fumes of the devil's music before he entered,
                to banish Jagger's pout and leer, the eighth-grade voo-
doo
        of Creedence Clearwater Revival, the spell-casting
of the year's one-hit wonders, briefly blessed as the glittering
        damned who'd bartered their souls for money or flesh.
                If I fell asleep before twelve, I might wake
        to his voice, tireless and rhythmic as the single vowel
of warning the red light on the radio tower called to passing planes.
        More than once I heaved awake from dreaming of nails
                being driven through hands and feet, choking
        in the airless fury of sulfur and brimstone, snakes noose-tight
around dying limbs while he launched into yet another cry for judg-
ment
        and apocalypse. Few things cheered him more than describing
                hell and pestilence. I thumbed the radio's small dial
        for Chicago or Nashville as I'd hitchhike one day to cities
that were only names until I got there. Throbbing guitars, bleeding
        harmonicas washed over me. Big-footed drums shook my sleep,
                although snakes still wove the edges of my dreams.

Entwined with every other listener and late night caller
riding the small hours, every truck driver boiling with speed,
          every lover insomniac with joy or longing,
               I sought an anthem to define the world beyond
          my postered room, his shade-tree town with its one
state road rolling in and heading back out. Outside my window,
          every house was dark. Even the street lights were dim, the four
way
               light on the corner burning for long minutes in each
direction.
          Flyover land, my friends who have moved to New York
or L.A. call this spider mass of towns tied together by roads that grow
          wider each decade, cable TV, radio songs, a stupid faith
               in the glamour of elsewhere and the goodness of the
place
          where we stand. Computers select tracks for radio stations now
and radio preachers, called pastors, their listeners flocks, host websites
          though their demons have the very same names.
               The need to be heard does not change. And if you flew
          above these dark counties you would see only a scatter of lights,
nothing
to map your way, the music joining them invisible.

NAMES THAT FORM ONE ABSENCE

Every few nights a drunk wants music
bad enough to curse or punch the jukebox,
stone-silent for years although its lights
still cast a thin carnival sequence
over tables where drunks have carved names
until one set of letters covers another,
all of them spelling absences endless
as thirst beer and whiskey will not quench.

This afternoon, one man sat alone
at a table, drinking water, shuffling
arrowheads he walked just-turned fields
to find, something he does each spring,
plucking stone tongues sharpened centuries ago
to say the one cold word of the past. Perhaps
be believed he could somehow arrange them
so the past would unlock, let music rise

out of stone, out of the silent jukebox.
Each year the fields are harder to walk,
the arrowheads fewer. And no stone will
carve the name of his particular absence
into wood. He left to put the arrowheads
on his wife's grave, mute testimony
to the failures of flesh, of water and stone.
When he returns, they will be gone.

He used to enter the church and kneel
to say her name, but today silence
and deep thirst send him back to the bar
where he drinks whiskey without water
until the tired stone of his tongue
rises into song that flies over
empty plains of prayer and absence
to meet the jukebox's stained lights.

TALISMAN

It was a painting bestowed on me
     by a roommate's old lover, a woman
a few years older than him or me, who
     would kill herself before turning thirty.
The painting itself was a blue rectangle
     divided by a stripe of green, then
a brown rectangle. Earth and sky.
     In the blue, which paled from turquoise
to nearly white as the eye moved upward,
     a wasp hovered, so outsized and detailed
nobody looked only once at the painting
     and looked away. It hung on my wall until
I no longer saw it, but I wondered sometimes
     about the square in the bottom half,
a mesh of muted colors swirling in the muddy brown,
     and deep within that pocket of color,
the outline of a wasp, blueprint
     for a body could just be seen.
Someone told me, or I read, that some insects,
     some wasps, burrow into the earth
to lay eggs in winter so the young emerge
     in spring fully grown. I lost the painting
or gave it away, and all the time it was
     before me rarely gave a thought
to the woman who gifted it to me,
     a woman so sad she made me angry.
Now the painting is gone, thus eligible
     to be invented, its blue or one
of its blues a match for the hive-thick coat
     she wore in winter, when wasps were buried
to deliver their pulpy eggs and die,
     their stings spent as the syringe
that fell from her fingers in the last second

she was alive, when the buzz of this world
fell away so she could hear the dying wasps:
    Remember how we came out of dark earth
and rose, more dangerous than smoke, wings
    delicate as the brush strokes painters use
to render our armed bodies luminous,
    thirsty all our short lives.

FROM *INVENTING CONSTELLATIONS*

(2012)

THE DEFINITIONS

"This thing is for life," says the movie crime boss to the one just induct-ed into "the family" in a spooky ritual involving blood and candles. The only light burning in this room is the TV, the sound turned low to let my family sleep. "For life," echoes the just made man.

§

The root of "family" is the Latin *familia,* which meant servants to a household.

§

My daughter brings home drawings of our family, the three of us with arms protruding from our heads, eyes too large to blink.

Sometimes she colors her face darker because "I'm brown and you're pink."

§

A blog I stumble across calls adoptive parents thieves. I type nine para-graphs in reply, delete them all.

§

A family is music: Kingston Trio songs sung off-key, a father's favorite radio station, the soundtrack to *South Pacific.* It's *turn that down* and *you call that music?* It is a mother and father in the kitchen dancing to a song they forgot they loved.

§

In 1788 "family man" was slang for a thief.

§

A family is a flock of butterflies whispering over an afternoon lawn, a herd of water buffalo knee-deep in river mud, a pride of lions chewing soft meat.

§

Her first day with us, she wept so endlessly I would have called back all the lawyers, the foster mother, erased the small mountain of forms, wiped our faces from our passports to let her sleep quiet in the place she knew. Now she asks the story of that day, prompts us to insert details left out from the last telling until the story is exactly as she wants to hear it.

§

This family speaks brutal fact.
This family speaks gesture and shadow.
This family needs argument before they can sing.
You learn the code when you learn language.

§

Planning the reunion: Frank isn't speaking to a once-favorite niece. No one should mention Jimmy's last rehab or relapse or talk politics with Ray. Someone needs to make a vegan dish for Megan and her fiancée. Jeff and Sherry will be bringing the kids from both marriages. Sonny wants to know if his band can play. There will be no time to rehearse.

§

Families are voices in other rooms, conversations that stop when you walk in, a television's gray noise low at night. There are dishes clattering in the kitchen, chairs scraping the floor. Songs half-heard through closed doors. Toilets flushing. Unnamed missions. A light that burns all night on an empty porch.

§

One afternoon after asking about her birth mother, Isabel draws a picture of herself in front of our house. "I'm leaving to live in my new house," she says.

§

I see my neighbor smoking on his back step, a moment of quiet outside a house clamoring with relatives who slam doors, yell from room to room, play the same CD over and over.

§

From the den my daughter calls, "Mama, it's our song," and for two minutes they are a single unit of joy, dancing to that inane song: "I'm so glad" *clap clap clap* "you're my family. I'm so glad" *clap clap clap.*

§

A family is a boomtown, the only nest of light for miles, its laws evolving with each new development. Shifts work around the clock, saloons never close and the streets fill with stories that mean nothing to anyone who doesn't live here.

§

Family began to mean "those connected by blood" in the 1660's. "In the family way" as a euphemism for pregnancy was first recorded in 1796.

§

We could not get in the family way. Now we ask how it could have been any other way.

§

Tonight on the edge of sleep, children hear songs whose words they will never forget, the songs their parents dance to wearing old smiles.

§

Coming in the front door, I hear Isabel's voice, see her run toward me, bend to meet this noise, this music, this song I keep singing in a house crowded by hope, furniture, our collected things, all of them, I hope, for life.

BLUE COLLAR

This blue shirt, slack on its hanger, waiting
to take the shape of my body, is not the blue collar
my father warned was waiting for me
if I continued to be confounded
                              by decimals and fractions.
Neither is it the ice-blue Oxford my father wore
on Fridays, his white shirts at the cleaners.
I knew the collars and the jobs he spoke of
on those nights when his voice loosened with a few drinks,
and he worked to explain to me
his theories of class and economics,
                              words
that slid by me like the rules of math
or grammar, my ears full of radio songs
and the stanzas of revolution I read
in underground papers my friends got
from older brothers.
                      They were the grease-mapped shirts
worn by the men who worked in the oil-dark cave
of the filling station owned by Billy Neal,
who called my dad "brother" and asked him what
the good word was. My father always had one.
They were the dark khaki shirts sweated through
by Mr. Anthony, the school janitor,
who never spoke, whose knack for fixing
what was broken trumped the bathrooms
he did not clean for weeks on end.
They were the frayed shirts with company logos
and names stitched over the pockets,
    worn
by my friends' fathers as they came home
from the bottling plant or the mill with no good words to say,
who opened sweating cans of beer and slowly
unlaced their shoes, mumbling half-sentences to their sons
and nothing at all to me.

PARENTHOOD AS CORRESPONDENCE COURSE

I'm dividing time between the video
     on Appropriate TV and scratching

equations meant to reveal exactly
     how much time with the spouse subtracts

from our estimated budgets for sleep
     and work. When that sum is discovered,

I'll restart the video and begin my essay
     on the use of inside and outside voice.

The wings of moths leave crescents, tiny commas
     and parentheses on the window. The pen slips

on the page, rights itself, continues
     its midnight-black calculations.

You are only as good as your last grade,
     and grades can be assigned

by any member of the faculty, which is
     composed, it seems, of anyone

who is not me. I almost said "save me,"
     but according to my transcript,

a pockmarked roster of failures and incompletes,
     I might be beyond saving.

To be sure, I've had my moments: acing
     the quiz on eating broccoli

in public. The talk about death.

But new assignments abandon

the syllabus. Fresh deadlines sprout like mold.
    No matter how I shave the figures,

I come up short on patience and time.
    Nothing to do but sigh and start again.

Crack a fresh notebook, uncap a pen.

TUNING

For Malcolm Holcombe

Because harmony is possible, for some it becomes commandment,
  and they train the ear
to the physics of the string, fussing till their instruments
  sound chords deep and true
as what vibrates in waves from deaf and distant stars
  to shiver the dime-speck
of light floating on every cup of coffee I've ever poured.
  But the same tiny lights
glow night-long on every electronic gadget I own,
  even the seldom-used guitar tuner
a friend sent. When a string is stretched into
  the right frequency,
the needle locks in, and a small green light glows
  soft as a blush. You can
move to the next one, then back to the beginning, until
  perfection delivers itself
as a set of diminished rewards. I once saw a band
  shamble onstage for
a second set long after midnight, and one guitar player asked,
  "Does anyone care
if we're in tune or not?" For years I thought I played badly
  because I could not tune
by ear. Now I have a machine to pull me in tune, and still
  my playing is
an out-of-time disaster. Most nights I leave the guitar
  in the case and listen
to recordings of players who have a chance of joy or discovery
  in their playing, who have
abandoned the drab memorization of this finger here, that one
  down there. When sun strikes
the proper angle through the window, each spark of dust claims
  a glowing, incandescent
as any of the unobtainable stars that freckle the sky, and when
  a finger bends

the right string in the right direction, a small fissure, crooked
        as a vein, deepens
in my heart, which is, for that moment, locked in harmony
        with all the other hearts
quickening in time to music which, like light, touches and moves,
        refusing to pause
even for the musician who know so well where to place his fingers
        it is no longer thought
that makes him bend a note just far enough to break a heart.

PARENTHOOD AS BAD THEOLOGY

I am becoming the sermon I promised
        I would not deliver, a sackclothed shadow,

caricature wielding the finger of admonition.
        Smoky entreaties, curly wisps of logic
no cartographer could unwind because they could not

be drawn on dirt or cut through trees and stone
        flow from my mouth until words vanish,

leaving only the empty bubbles cartoonists draw
        above the heads of their characters before
they give them something funny to say.

To lose the religion of punch line and caption,
        I need to remember no one crossed the walked-thin

carpet of my childhood church believing
        in instant salvation a second time. Instead I see
scars the savage mill blade left on the pews

where I sat, feel the weight of thin-leafed hymnals,
        how easy it was to believe in unmoving eternity

in a room where time seemed to kneel and never rise.
        The stained glass windows never showed us
the weather, their depictions of saints and apostles,

of Jesus cradling the lamb as off-kilter and unrealistic
        as the cartoons I still read each morning.

She won't need my testimony to know I fevered
        on Sundays, hoping my parents might
decide to skip church that day. She already understands

the arbitrary laws of families. A few more years
      of watching me wave my arms and babble

like a drunken cartoon character, empty circles
      of air floating from my mouth, and she will know
exactly the words she does not want to say.

BLINDFOLD

Maybe the blindfold is not meant
as kindness for the condemned
like the choice of a final meal
or the last cigarette, a pleasure
meant to block awareness
of what's coming. Instead it keeps
the living from seeing how
the eyes throttle with light
or glaze at the moment of impact
before the body empties into death.
In this age of performance, even an autopsy,
final audition of the body's efficiency,
is theater. A TV doctor explains
how the flanges of the famous chest
are opened like curtains, the routines
of the reliable duo, systole and diastole,
the shuttle cocking of artery and vein,
the blood's drifting clouds of toxins
all are measured and named,
no chance for curtain call
or final bow. In the film
I found on the internet and watched
because I started and could not stop
the killers, not the condemned, wore masks.
He knelt before them as they read
their proclamations in a language
he was captive long enough to know
in fragments. His face a blank
of pure misery, glossed with sweat,
his hair twisted and on end,
some composure kept him still.
Perhaps he'd seen enough movies,
was American enough to believe
in last-second rescues, the hero
who kicks in the door, guns blazing.

Maybe he believed this
routine humiliation between
tea and afternoon prayers,
a ritual meant to be so frightening
that when water was thrown on him
or he was kicked, their laughter
let him breathe once more.
But the reading ended and one
of the masked men produced a long knife.
There was nothing swift nor spectacular
about what followed. Bodies wrestled
across the floor. Deep inside the scrum
started noise too high-pitched to be a scream,
noise I'd never heard a human make.
When the head was displayed,
it was no longer human, but something
molded from plastic and left too long
in the back seat of a car on a hot day.
If you watch this once, you will not
watch it again. In this world,
beauty and terror coax the same tears,
the voice of fear has no words,
the victim's face is a trophy.
But morning still happens.
I get up, make coffee, walk the dog, things
I can do with my eyes closed.
Not until I read the paper or listen
to the news does the world take shape.
Some refuse the blindfold,
but most are grateful for a darkness
granted by a cloth so ordinary
it might have dried last night's dishes,
then wiped the empty table free
of crumbs and ashes.

PARENTHOOD AS ONE VERSION OF THE AFTERLIFE

How you get here is how you get here.
                                        Some arrive
silent, smug in the glow of an executed plan.
Others limp or shamble in, stunned as the occupants

of a wreck who, standing beside a car crumpled
as tinfoil, cannot stop uttering half sentences:

the rain. Weak-as water brakes. The tree.
But whether this is a well-crafted destination
or one more stop on calamity's highway,

dwelling in this new landscape will not be
what we thought. So this unmapped terrain bestows

a rough equality over all its citizens,
paralyzed by the expectation that they must be
decisive as battlefield commanders, yet patient

as supplicants who wait to be taken through
the brassy lungs of heaven's gates or cast

into the cloudy fires of hell. The life behind
claims no shadow, our unchilded beings
featureless as marble. Small details—

a shirt I once owned, a meal, the name, a movie's title—
belong to a past no longer completely mine.

Flickering through memory's bland weather, the voice
of a neighbor who, after a glowing and swollen pregnancy,
whispered, "It's really weird to have a kid."

That kid would be almost grown now,
a shadow-casting citizen of a world that started over

the first night our daughter was with us,
and I lay awake as they slept, trying to plan
each of the small and unknown eternities before us.

PRAYER FOR THE IMPONDERABLES

There we are, the sky executing
       its slow pirouette,
me walking the dog, looking up through
clear miles of night,
      an uninvited guest
spying on a party that commenced
long before I did not receive an invitation,
that will continue
     after I have stolen
back down the long drive, my feet noisy
in the gravel, after dark has erased
my body and all the music
and laughter I am not permitted.

§

One night the end of day will be
the end of all days,
     at least the ones
I have been allowed a hand in.
The sun will pull
     its crimson thumbprint
down my window a final time,
      an organ
will sound a long downward drone.
       It will be—
and this might be my last thought—a song
inappropriate for the occasion.

§

We are here so briefly.
     No sense in thinking
about it. No end of thinking about it.
This is one reason to make stories.

We could
look into the campfire and chant,
                    sparks rising,
stars the color of glass, a million nameless bones
buried beneath us
                    but naked fact offers
no comfort, no feigned resolution.

§

Back and forth.
            The brush gliding boards scraped
almost bare, then repainted in hopes of holding on
a few winters more.
            The houses listed,
brick piers crumbling, nails sighing loose, air
and light chiseling through boards gone
out of plumb.
            When the old man who lived
in the one where I was working alone, the rest
of the crew gone for cigarettes or looking
                        at another job,
offered me water, I stood in his thin hallway,
stared through missing boards
                    at the bare ground.
A song on his kitchen radio promised
we have a home in heaven waiting.
                    Oooh whee, oooh whee.

§

Fifty one years and I still believe
                    something
is about to happen.

Southern winter. Grass brittle
with night frost,
　　　　　and sleep feels like surrender
to what it necessary and rare.
　　　　　　　　Soon, too soon,
a child will tug me awake, a day will
　　　　　　　　　　　groan into motion,
and there will be no time to ponder
　　　　　　　　　　the grim subtractions
and how we work to ignore them. Nor should there be.

§

So hold on, old universe.
　　　　　　　　You too, sweet daughter.
I am running out of words for things
　　　　　　　　　like stars.
Or love. The imponderable will always
　　　　　　　　　await us.
And somewhere before us, at the end
of all our thinking, each name will be written.
But not today.
　　　　　And not tomorrow. And not
as long as I can keep the small breath
in transit, feeding the engines
that click and burn,
　　　　　　　then exiting on vapors
of invisible fires that aspire,
helplessly, to the clarity of stars.

FROM *MUSIC IN SMALL TOWNS*
(2014)

SELF PORTRAIT AS A MOVING VAN ON FIRE

Boys in small towns love fire, and these boys know
every town is small. Everywhere I lived, we performed
the ritual of matches, coaxed budding flame
with pine straw and twigs until branches
as long as our arms, longer, became fire
and its caustic aftermath.
                              Because boys will not
say what they love, they weave a language
in the blue heart of flame, where their offerings
vanish into mounded ash, die into nests
where only a few coals wink and smolder. At dawn,
the two boys who never had to be home would rise,
push handfuls of sticks into stirred embers,
try to burn the night again.

§

In the desert, a friend and I built a fire
that brought a helicopter sweeping a spotlight
over the ground. We said nothing, just ran
far enough to be hidden, fast enough for this to be
no more than a story for the next place we went.
                                             I knew
so little I had no answer for the well-wishing
of a teacher on my last day in his class.
                                   I did know
nothing vanished even in fire. Clocks would shrug
through their hours and all the things
whose names I had learned would continue
while I rode a thousand miles in a new direction
to find a new school, a new house waiting
to be filled by our dry furniture, the matches
I saved in a drawer and would not strike.

§

We drove east. And on the second night passed
a burning 18 wheeler, a corridor of flame
on the road's shoulder. Lights throbbed
like frantic hearts. A silver curve of water rose,
falling into the hollow center
of the fire.
         For a moment we believed
our lives burned in that truck,
and all our fears were one fear.
When we stopped that night, when
it was time to sleep, I could only see
the burning walls of the van, how they peeled
into layers and fell into the gravity of fire.

§

Nothing of ours burned that night.
We moved into our new house
and have been left to time's burning, which is slower
and more thorough. I still love fire. And know
all the reasons to fear it.
           Sometimes I wake
in this house where I've lived longer
than I've ever lived anywhere, my body racing
with its dreams of fire gone wrong.
Then I rise, walk over yesterday's ash-gray dust
to make coffee and wait for the dark van
that carries day to arrive and begin stacking
its unburned furniture on my yard.

LOVE SONG FOR ELECTRICITY

For the first time I thumbed a humming E string
        and heard the note, not hollow against my belly
but barking from a red-lit amp four feet away,
        the wood floor trembling with the sound, for the pierced
barb of feedback, the white flash of distortion,
        for the first wax cylinder's hissy recording of Edison
growling "Mary Had A Little Lamb," thanks.
        For the saddle bend, the pulled wire, the three-way
switch, for the years I spent learning to harness
        the lightning song of electricity behind walls,
for the lay-offs, the Friday I was fired and walked home,
        the stark building growing taller behind me,
I will not say thanks, but those are the lessons
        my fingers remember when I change a switch
or when I replaced the failing light fixtures in my kitchen.
        For Peter Coyote giving away 1200 LP's because
he thought he would never live with electricity again,
        for candles that make every room a cave,
for the fat wicks of lanterns, for campfires, for oil
        and coal and the cords of logs I have split,
without you I would not love the salt-colored light
        this lamp casts over my shoulder as much as I do.
For the kool aid, the strobe, the nightmare wash
        of black light, for the tape and the tape loop,
for the recordings and the gaps in recordings,
        how different would this present be without you?
For the light that answers the commands of the switch
        at 3 a.m., for music rolling from these speakers
to soothe the room, for rooms suddenly rich with light
        after a two-day power outage, for Edison again,
for Tesla, for the gods of alternating and direct current,
        even the snake of the short circuit that bites
the careless hand or finger, for the hundred watt bulb,

the fluorescent, for the rivers dammed
so the southeast could be flooded with light, I offer
an unamplified praise to what is plugged in and singing,
song we notice only in its absence,
the sudden silence, dark of the unfinished note.

MUSIC FROM SMALL TOWNS

No one is nearby to give lessons, but boys willing
        to needle L-O-V-E and H-A-T-E into their knuckles long
before

they sniff the damp walls of a jail cell would not listen
        if there were. Drummers learn rhythm by chopping wood,

guitar players find a few chords and sniff nail polish
        or glue before practice. Since they have nothing

to sing about, that is what they sing. The secret is playing
        long enough to allow the houses where they sleep, the stores

where they buy magazines and gum, the parking lots where fathers
        or brothers ground them in the harmonies of pedal

and clutch, all to find room to breathe inside that nothing.
        The ones who have not driven those streets hear

red lights and blood, car wrecks, crazy sisters, the cost
        of living a life you know you will never understand.

Dust and pollen film windshields, a tire sighs flat.
        Imperfection might prove one form of salvation.

On the sidewalk, a bird that broke its neck
        flying into a window washed too clean.

Empty chords ring out, called for
        by natives and strangers when the runaway sons

glare and play their version of a place
        that didn't know it had a name before it became a song.

SELF PORTRAIT IN THE AMNESIA OF FIRE

I am not the flicker of fire
                    on the hill behind my house,
little phoenix egg, tiny starling of flame, finding
shape and vanishing, thoughts fragmenting
in every wind shift.
                I have surrendered
such fluidities of motion, such refusals
to be satisfied, those hungers
                       so insistent
they forget what they consume.

§

When gravity or noise
                twists me awake,
I can lie for hours for hours, caught in the symphonies
of regret the brain composes—at 3 a.m.
no one remembers triumph—until
a spur-shaped pain kicks deep in the shoulder
to be answered by a pin-sharp twinge
in the ankle or knee.
              Memory is
one reason to have a body,
           despite pain
and its long insistence on history,
its need to show just where
                the body has been,
no matter what secrets we wish
flesh would keep.
           We could not be
wholly of fire, a present tense so endless
it will not mourn even our demise.

Like most, I live in the uneasy rapture
of fire and memory.

§

To the man on the hill, huddled
over his little cone of forgetting,
I am a lit window, a shadow
made completely of the moment.
                              Or I am
a silhouette inside a burning
that does not change.
                    I always wanted
to be more than a fleeting ache,
thumbprint on a glass, a circle
of cold ash.
            It will be for those
who count the artifacts our lives become
to say whether or not I succeeded
though I suspect
                    we are mostly small images
and their erasures,
                    flames consumed
by their own motion, facts in search
of a language that can weave them
into something able to remember
the stubborn forgetting
of fire and the man beside it.

WE LIVED BY THE RIVER

For Mark Kemp

Amazing how tame it sounds now
                                        that it is history,
no longer mired in the chaos of becoming. When
punk moved into the house we rented by the river,
each silence meant a new clash over the turntable.
                                        The record
with pink and green letters blazed over a black and white
of man swinging a guitar like an axe
                                        made the sound
of old palaces becoming dance halls.
"Balloon rock," I'd sneer.
                        "Radio static," and Mark would bounce
"The Guns of Brixton" a notch higher.
                                        Mosquitoes rose
from the dark water
                        in blood-sniffing clouds.

There was little to believe in that summer but the constant mosquitoes.
I'd argued my way out of faith
                                        in God, politics, or classrooms.
Even the soft boundaries of books seemed to crumble.
The dirt crusted under my nails,
                                        the blood-moons
my pliers bit into my hands, my angry pride
in working a ten-hour day sustained me. Rock was dying or dead
and I would not trust musicians younger than me
to deliver
                        what the junkie millionaires of my childhood
never could.
                        It was the last year my nights were slow enough
to spend hours arguing with Mark about our record collections.

Time fills time.
          Mark and his records moved
at the end of summer. A few years later, he was reviewing records
in New York City; I was writing poems.
                    And a few weeks ago,
I stood under a tree to watch Mark marry.
                        One summer night,
years after our summer by the river, I found a black cassette
marked "London Calling," on the floor of a closet,
a forgotten piece of my wife's past.
                   I pushed "play"
and my arguments with time vanished in the jab and pull
of the guitars,
          the stop-march cadence of drums.
That guitar swinging downward still holds
                   in the moment
before breaking as though the river, for a second, could
cease its muddy flow and allow us time to know
what is worth saving and what is not.

ANGELS OF THE NEW ROAD

If we have more than one version of hell,
                                            and we do,
one must be the labor of the night crew
repaving the interstate,
                            who stand
ankle-deep in hot asphalt and drag it level
with rakes before stepping out of the way
so a steamroller can press it
into a road's seamless mat.

All of this in fume-thick air, taunted
by bugs pulled to the static glaze of halogen lights
kept burning by motors that choke and roar,
                                            their exhaust
brewed with asphalt's raw stink in the soup-warm air
while cars rip by, their speed an echo
                            of the hollow
deep in the center of the body.

Tell me you have not seen them and nearly swerved
into the wrong lane, ignored
                            by those men
whittled to bare function
by work that erodes them so thoroughly,
                                            their task shapes them
into efficiency.
                    There is none of the grab ass
and loud talk, none of the woman-calling
of a daytime crew,
                        only the small lit circle
of labor, only work stretched so far before them
that progress is an illusion,
                                like the painters
of that famous bridge who complete the north end

on Friday and on Monday cross the bay
to begin the south end.
Don't the moon-glare of lights that throw no shadow
and the wraiths of steam fogging upward
make you slow, staring long enough

                                              to be grateful

for the surface you ride on, the speed
that lets you and those men vanish
in dark and heat fog,
                        angels
of burning asphalt, rolled under, resurrected
in milky steam,
                        in the shine
of wing-speck and broken membrane,
of glassy motes visible only when
sun's full weight shines on the new road?

BIRDS ARE ONE MUSIC OF THE WORLD

For Don Adcock, 1926-2011

Because they are beautiful
and small, with brassy songs
and feathers that host the entire
range of visible color, I could
listen or watch without any need
to know their names. My wife reads
markings and colors, can tell
one from the other, which is native
and which migrating or lost.
Perhaps I should not be content
with how little of the world
I can name. When my friend's hands
no longer let him play flute
or sort out chords on the piano,
he read in a chair beside
a floor-to-ceiling window. Soon
he knew the species and song
of each bird crowding the feeders
in his yard. Sometimes he would scat
a few bars of bird song
the way he scatted jazz licks,
music replacing music, his song,
from a body slowly learning
the inhospitalities of gravity,
imitating those smaller bodies
still blessed with music and flight.

POEM THAT WANTS TO BE A POSTCARD TO CHRIS BUCKLEY

This is no weather for walking.
Cold webs of drizzle stitch
the blusters of early morning,
but the dog, caught in the failures
of an aging body, whines
to go out at 3 am, at 5.
Coming in from one of those walks,
I flip on the light, find again
a postcard you sent, uncovered
this afternoon while I searched
for stamps.
           Because nothing stays
where I put it or think I put it,
I find your occasional cards
tucked in drawers, falling out of books,
words to scan again as the coffeemaker
brews a bad answer to a night
robbed of sleep.
           After pouring coffee,
I open your newest book, the one
you inscribed as though you and I
play the netless oddity
poetry has become equally well.
And breathed again the endless dust,
the eucalyptus and lemon
of your native state, a place
I've barely visited but believe
I know because I can read.
           Once
my wife and I left a hotel filled
with writers to find some lunch.

While we chewed chips and salsa
in the booth of a Mexican restaurant,
we eavesdropped on a table filled
with writing students. When one said
her friend wanted to date a poet,
my wife whispered, "No, she doesn't"
so fiercely I thought of the mockingbird
in our yard that dives at me, screaming
an intruder from its nest,
                              and I wondered
if I should take up essays
or science fiction. At a lake
near my house, a place where
I might have walked the dog when
she was young enough to feel
spring rising in her bones,
someone has placed a camera
so anyone who wishes can go
to a web site and watch two eagles
hatch their young.
                    Each time
I dial in, the screen could be
a postcard, the nest is so still,
the sky so empty. It takes
a special talent to scan
the landscape and love what is not there,
the way we love the unwritten
or half-written poem, the vanished
hangouts of our youth or the way
one girl dreams love for a poet
or her notion of a poet.
                          Last night,
I read your poem that pretended
it wanted to be a postcard
to Gerald Stern, who might be

recipient of more epistolary poems
than anyone since God. Last week,
in a store stacked and crowded
by second hand texts, I found
a copy of *Lucky Life*, a book
I had not read since college,
and I spent an afternoon deep
in the prayed-over landscape
of those poems that struggle
in the margin between the woods
and the road, half-civilized
berms where I spent my boyhood.
Many of Stern's poems might have fit
on a postcard.
                Yours will not.
Neither will this one. I will finish
what there is to write this evening
and spend more nights and weekends
adding, subtracting, weaving
into the chaos of this poem
scraps of news, half-memories of walking
the dog when it could still negotiate
steep switchbacks, the free verse
on the back of a card announcing
the engagement of an unseen girl
and her poet. Then I'll crease it,
send it to the address stamped
in one corner of your card,
imagine its arrival.
                I'm good at that.
We've all imagined lives
for one another. We've all steered
into curves too fast and made
a lifetime's worth of promises
to the gods of speed and gravity,

different from the ones offered
to the gods of upright walking
and slow reading.
              Breathless,
we ask only to be pulled
to safety one last time.
We've all studied the wind, wished
across the great distances it covers
across acres of golden dust
for the strength and faith of birds
on their fledgling flights,
and that those of us watching
be forgiven for a moment
the aging bodies, the books
read and forgotten and the little
read once and saved forever.

THE SWEET DRIVE OF HISTORY

For the dinosaurs first, who rose and roamed humid earth,
whose sandwich-sized brains and heavy limbs fell prey
to collisions of climate and time, whose naked remains
were bone, then sludge, then cooked deep in rock to become
the gunk dredged up from sand and refined to fuel
the dying growls that wind now in the chorus line of cars
on the wide road behind my house. For the boys who could
spend hours describing the cars they would drive, the tricked-out
engines, the tuck-and-roll interiors, the paint like cold fire,
who drew pictures of Camaros, Mustangs and GTOs in the margins
of math tests, who pretended to know motors by their sounds,
who vanished under car hoods, eager for the baptisms of grease
that let the hymns of a torqued-up engine rev the afternoon air.
For my first car, however many parts it rusts in now,
for its 396 that guzzled fifty cent gallons of gas and was pulled
from under the hood before I was done signing the papers
giving the car to the junkyard. For the brokedown engine,
the driving wheel, for four on the floor and the double clutch,
for the sweet cargo of language whose passengers we are
and the litanies of repair: the flywheels and fan belts,
tie rods and hoses, the pumps, suspensions, catalytic converters,
all the born-to-fail-sooner-or-later pieces held
in the vibrating house of metal. For the Terraplane, the Rocket 88,
the Old 55 and Sweet Little 66, for the Little Red Corvette,
the Long White Cadillac and Joplin's Mercedes Benz,
for the throat-song of carburetor, the oiled harmony
of clutch and gear, the smooth acceleration that makes
the dark tenor of the road hum under tires.
For the real breakdowns: one night in the fisted hills
of north Arkansas, driving thirty slow miles at a time,
waiting twenty minutes for the engine to cool and driving
another thirty. Another highway, another state, the hood raised
in the universal sign of helplessness, geysers of steam towering

in the baking air, merciless sun burning the concert tickets
in our pockets to ash, to less than ash. For stopping
every fifty miles to pump air into a leaking tire, for buying
oil by the case, for the car that carried me home from
the junkyard and all the cars I have driven or ridden in since until
this afternoon in the not-quite-new Subaru, Leonard Cohen
or Wilco singing over the engine's shortcomings. For the ghost
in the machine, the noise that answers no prayers,
for the sourceless love of motion driving us from the car lot
to the rusted hulks squatted on cinderblocks, last secretions
of oil drooling into dust, into hardpan and sandy dirt,
leaking through veins and fissures that lead any matter
small enough to leak into earth into the chambers where
centuries of heat and pressure have alchemized bodies and bones
into the sluggish ooze that has launched slippery fortunes
and turned the wheels carrying us past the roadside memorials
of those claimed by speed or a careless moment, the plastic flowers
that do not wilt or move in the endless breeze our traffic stirs.

FROM *THE NEXT PLACE*

(2017)

THE GOSPEL OF LEAVING

Before we knew the world, we wanted to know the limits
of the world. We plundered The Gospel of Weather

whose single verse is motion, a page rewritten each day,
its inaccuracies ingrained more deeply than its truths.

We followed the false paths of sidewalks marked
with initials of children dead or long-vanished until

we crossed the highway to red dirt trails leading
up to the dull pocket of lake. The town went invisible

from there, save a few church steeples, rising singular
as the hands of the girl who bowed her head at lunch

to bless the invisible steam rising from corn, tasteless beans,
sticks of freezer-burned fish. We followed footpath

and smoke-drift from there up into the tree line
to the mouths of the caves, veins of dark and gravity

we dared ourselves to enter but never did. Pine needle
and leaf-corpse piled dense beneath the trees so the dirt

never dried. And we never walked far enough to leave
evidence of man-life behind us. There was always a pint

leaning empty under a tree, a twisted cigarette pack.
A pair of names shining, new scars in the brown flesh

of a tree. Always a sign to say our lives were never
our own. Above us, the crest of a hill like the promise

of afterlife though we knew that if we topped that hill,
there would be another valley, a steeper hill to climb,

a progression proving that we needed to leave this place
as soon as we were able. As we descended, our shadows stretched

long enough to blend with each other. The gold courthouse dome
emerged, burning in this rare angle of sun. If I believed

in a church-quiet and eventless heaven, empty of all
save joy, I might have asked some future saint—Shakespeare,

Dante, Bill Evans—to ease my passage. But how long will anything,
even rapture, last? We return to what we know.

and most of us learn so little that we walk the clatter
of dirt life and its ten million discords until

we have no choice but to love, even though every descent
is rehearsal, a goodbye we do not own yet.

HOW DIFFERENT A LIFE CAN BE

For Jeff Hardin

Spring seems, finally, to have a toehold here,
but I'll tell you, buddy, I still can't shake
winter's hibernations from bones or blood.
An unspoken fact of age is how slowly
the body allows changes, even the ones
that are inevitable. I still long after
early dark and long sleep. This morning,
I woke on the couch at 4 a.m., the TV still
spinning the nonsense I'd nodded off to.
Tomorrow I'll haul out the lawnmower
and cut the spongy grass, which seemed
to grow an inch every day this week.
The way my daughter has grown beyond
any imagining I had that first frantic day
when she was placed, crying, in my arms.
Perhaps one reason I'm reluctant to see
the turns of seasons is my fear
of seeing her grow beyond needing me.
It's a truth I did not understand
the first day I took her to pre-school,
when she still could barely walk,
and all I knew of families I could write
on the palm of my left hand. When
we were waiting for her—it seems
like another life now—people would tell us
they were adopted or a sibling or spouse had been.
But when you wrote that you were,
it opened a space in the universe
where I had never stepped before
because I know how much you love the place
you grew up, the place you live now,
how its trees whisper into spring leafing
while flowers flare along property lines. It's hard
to fathom how different a life can be.
I've seen enough of the lives I might have had

to be grateful for this one. I suspect
you have as well. Tomorrow, when I'm done
cutting the grass, the air will be rich
with its damp green. I'll sit on my porch
without wanting to go anywhere else,
settling into what might be our greatest task:
to live this life as though we could imagine no other.

GUARDIAN

I, who was absent from the coupling that made you,
          who, on the day of your birth, stood unsuspecting,
my shadow a simple blank, a self I can't help seeing

          as empty now, I will forever feel the ghost-membrane
of that woman—a girl, really— and the young man who
          who made you and then, in sacrifice too great for human praise

trusted you to strangers on the thin rope, the pious
          assurance that the child could be delivered to a life of class-
rooms,
of air conditioners, the milk and vegetables we can offer.

It is no small thing to make a child. Or to raise one.
          The week after bringing you home, I sat bolt upright,
cradling you in the position that would let you sleep.

If I nodded into my own half-dream, if I slipped off
          my moorings, your screams tore both of us back
to wakefulness. Your appetite was for the soft organs,

the tarnished lungs, the recalcitrant liver, the long mile
          of intestine before you reach the underside of the heart, which
beats
too soft for our notice though mine must have hummed some trance
for you when your sweat-humid face pressed my skin, as though what
lay under

could be tasted, taken like communion wafers between the lips,
like crumbs of ice I gave you once when you fevered, unable to sleep,

stranded beyond any real comfort I could give. No longer guardian
        of sleep, I could only whisper the reassurances I crooned
on the plane from Guatemala when you screamed with the pain

of an ear infection we didn't know you had. I felt your forehead
        as I always do, reflex of every parent against
the fear that lies, live as electricity, in our bodies. After you wept

into damp sleep, I lay beside you, blood heavy as tar, body sluggish
        and primed for a butcher. The fever would course through you
as they all do, your body a way station, a port where

passengers without tickets dream new destinations. Before
        I was used to saying your name, when you were a smile
in photographs, before I coaxed you with fruit or spoonfuls

of soft egg, it was clear you would be no footnote
        or happy ending, but a story built to parallel mine,
the story I can only believe I was born to tell.

ISAAC, AFTERWARD

Once the ties were cut, while the ram coughed
    its last blood through the hole in its throat,
he rose from the stone altar, found his frayed tunic
    where it had fallen. Above the ram, his father
worked to empty the stomach cavity, the glistening
    blue intestines, the pink heart and wing-shaped lungs,.
He would not turn to see his son. The angel was gone,
    leaving only the suddenly foreign desert
the son had known from birth. His shadow burned
    against stone and vanished when he moved.
Vanished as he would have vanished. Now, he thought,
    would come new words, but his tongue lay
thick as wood his father had gathered for the pyre,
    all language dissolved in the blue distance
of horizon he had closed his eyes on minutes before.
    And no word came from his endlessly praying
father, the longest silence he remembers from
    the old man whose body has long seemed a chamber
echoing piety and aphorism. Blood still furious
    in his veins, he wondered about the journey home,
the ruined faith in his father's eyes. How long before
    he decided the angel was wrong, that a son's blood
must be spilled to wash sin? Over a low fire, his mother
    will stir a pot of bulgur and lentils. She is sure
her prayers have no resonance, but she says them,
    her faith a weight more certain than the children
who grew inside her heavy as stones. Her son knows
    what has been subtracted, what lives inside
the blood that rises, unspilled, in his belly.
    Now fire rises to take hold of the wood. The best meat
will be offered to the flames with prayers. The father works,
    never saying what he understands, that a father's life
is one mistake following another, that men dwell for years
    in the houses their fallen intentions build.

There will never be words to pull loose the nails,
        to sort the blade from flesh, to explain his life
to a son who, after tonight, will never sleep without a knife,
        who looked up at him with the shock the ram felt
bleeding at the center of a world going dim, bewildered
        at faith that asks such sacrifice.

READING OBITUARIES IN A STRANGE TOWN

No saying the means of their passing,
  these citizens of a strange tribe, too many

younger than I am this morning where
  I drink coffee and hold off the heavy dust

time dresses in by skimming the news
  in a town I never saw before today.

No unraveling these stories. Blood curses,
  I want to say, and spells that turn

the moon sour. Serpents electric
  with poison that brooks no cure.

Ancestral daggers, honed to stop the work
  of treacherous hearts. We need to believe

a wilderness waits, dark and wild, inside
  the places we visit. Something must linger

in shade, saying not our names,
  for we are strangers here, but older sounds,

calls we respond to without knowing
  exactly what we say. That shade

stretches all the way to our door,
  so we enter the safe light of our homes

to find a newspaper folded in our gear
  and hold it, wondering why

we saved such a thing.

THE SILENCE OF DISAPPEARING TRAINS

If drone was not a family of echoes circling the stone lungs
of cathedrals for centuries, I might swear it was born
in the iron bellows of train whistles, a come-all-ye invented

to warn of the train's presence in town, especially after
midnight, its rattle already enough to pierce
the thin bubble of my sleep, before the miles-long note

ascended the same upward sweep that washed from steel guitars
in the country songs my father loved. A few miles north,
the trains would shake across the skeletal bridge built to chain

the two banks of the Etowah. By then I would be fully awake,
alone with my fear of the morning's quiz on the periodic table,
material I had ignored, leaving me the honed recitals of failure,

cadences as familiar to me as the river must feel
to its rock and sand beds. The river, like the train, knew its course
and did not vary. Hard calculation for a town

where variation and motion seemed forever in short supply.
In our alley-thin lives, adventure meant blood or police cars,
meant events accelerated to a pace beyond our want

or control. It would be a while before physics told me
that motion is the single constant of our lives. Even inside us,
cities, tiny empires, rise and wash away, hordes of bacteria migrate,

the mostly reliable pistons of heart and pulse hammer
while skin loosens, lost chemicals hiss and froth. Pain camps
where it pleases and moves on at the insolent pace

of the movie tramp rousted from sleeping in an orchard,
sauntering off, pockets full of stolen fruit, at a pace that announces
he knows the clock measuring our existence has no numbers,

at least none that matter. I didn't see any such knowledge hidden
in the chart the teacher covered the next morning.
We turned the test over and began, never suspecting

that particles too fast and small to know were shooting through
the air, through the tops of our desks, the blackboards and maps,
the stringy meat of our bodies, all the illusory solids of the world,

binding us to the ever-widening universe as they moved
to the space between stars, between bridge and water, to motion
that continues the way rivers continue, that continues

whether we find ways to measure it or just believe it so.
Motion we never feel unless we sense it on some rare mornings
inside the breath between sleep and waking, mineral pulse

drawing us toward the outbending walls of the universe,
into the lazy present tense that is all breath of time have
to offer us. On a few lucky mornings, you might

roll toward a body likewise filled with infinity
and rolling toward you, the two of you learning again
how lovemaking offers one way of resolving time,

each motion invented to linger but bearing you both
to the inevitable end and the geological sadness
of bodies when they are still again.

But all of that was before me when I lay awake
in the silence of disappearing trains, knowing only that
I did not know what elements made the world.

VISITATION

In that house that could only be heated one room at a time,
where the bathroom floor was rotted through & camouflaged
by layers of slowly cracking linoleum, grace was a tenant

in another zip code, a place visible only by swallowing
odd-colored capsules or some blessing of the body.

We never believed it could enter as easily as the bird
that sailed in through the front door one morning and bumped
from room to room, wings and claws scrabbling streaked windows

as it darted for light, away from our waving arms & broomsticks,
the round vowels we sang, urging it to exit before it was forced
to remain trapped here with us. The family my mother hired

to paint our house when I was eleven all arrived in one truck,
the body mostly rust and pain, that swayed on its broken suspension
for a full minute after they parked. One morning, the father was

not there. He'd been bitten in church, the oldest son explained,
his glass eye angled toward some unused portion of paradise.

It was the first time I knew that animals could be
harbingers of that other, hidden life. Years after, the bird flew
back out the front door and vanished into the green heaven

of trees, I learned that a bird in the house prophesied that death
would soon come and find a place to sit under that roof.

But a few will vow that birds will enter only chosen homes
to fly among those with souls as welcoming as the sky.
I'm not sure what is needed for hands willing to pick up

the slick muscle of a snake and pray, but the body must be
so emptied of fear that what lives inside it will fly,

heedless and seeing into shadows framed by a door,

certain only that it can navigate what waits there
and escape into the cicada-rattle of the day
and the nights all our prayers will never fill.

LEAVING AN AA MEETING DURING A SNOWSTORM

It took a lot of coffee to wash away
       the fear of nights that dropped on black wings

into my last year of drinking.
       That fear, like everything, had its time

and passed. In meetings, I drink a small cup,
       sit without shaking, and speak

when I am asked. A silence like church
       inhabits me then, a silence like this snow

making a castle of night, a structure
       grand and endless, soft gathering

that hides the world long enough
       that its vanishing might let us believe

once more in rebirth, in fresh beginnings.
       Once I heard a truck driver's story

of being stranded by snow in a high pass
       of mountains. He left the icy cab

of the truck and walked for help until
       he no longer felt his body,

until he heard voices urging him
       to lie under dark pines and rest.

Soon, they promised, the cold would end.
       The trucker was not a drunk

sharing his story in a meeting,
      but I knew those voices. They told me

to sit at the bar a little longer and order
      one more drink. Home would be there

when I got there. If she couldn't understand,
      I was better off without her.

Ahead of me, a car slants into a slow slide
      and my blood throttles with electricity

no espresso will summon. I steer
      the car toward my night-filled house,

driving slow and easy, getting home
      once again the hardest part of the night.

THE WORLD OF WHISKEY

For Tom House

"If the river was whiskey and I was a duck

Might swim to the bottom, never come up"

—Traditional blues lyric

Understand. The world was
whiskey once, and dive we did,
seeking the shifting bottom
of dreams we believed were ours
to offer anyone with
an ear or a need to listen.
Mired in sand and duck weed,
we stared up through ambered
layers, through the floating
of broken chairs, undreamed lines,
searching the ice-melted
memory of sun. We were
a long time drifting to shore,
not sure we could stand
when we got there. But deep
in the old woods, voices sang
and we learned we could hear
enough to know what they said.
And as we slipped into
the first fringes of tree-shade,
we found ourselves wanting
to sing for the first time
in a long while, all fear
of drowning shaken from us
as long as we could follow
those songs to the unbottled
waters of their birth.

MEMORIAL DAY

I was a patriot when I drank.
        Hours at the bar primed me
to storm the beachfronts, throw bottles
        into intersections, lay siege
to frozen food aisles. I wanted
        a toy republic with flags
and my own stool at the V.F.W.
        Today, I'm trying to learn why
flags have dipped to half-mast.
        They've lowered for presidents
and actresses, but the only tragedy
        worthy of the name recently
has been a random shooting spree
        in another corner of the country,
an occurrence remarkable only because
        the shooter left a video
to explain his actions. Today,
        I reminded my wife of a Memorial Day
when Malcolm lit a block of fireworks,
        and one nearly shot into
the tailpipe of a running car.
        That was the Fourth of July,
she told me. I've forgotten more days
        than I will ever remember.
Today I dismantled the slow-dying tree
        in our front yard, thinking about
the Merwin essay about unchopping
        a tree. Then I thought about
his new book of poems, which I didn't like
        as much as some of his others.
And other books I liked or didn't
        while the chainsaw chewed limbs,
some green, some veined with rot.

My friend Bryan once felled a tree
with a few shots from his rifle. The one
        useful thing he learned
in the Navy, he said. The last time
        I held a gun, it was a single shot .22
my brother used to teach his daughters
        how to shoot. We aimed
at paper targets but might have hit
        some trees. Even the five year olds
took a few shots. I wasn't thinking of guns
        when a branch fell opposite
of the way I expected and hit
        my shoulder and sent my glasses flying.
It took a long while to find them
        among the debris Merwin says
we must gather crumb by crumb
        if we are to unchop the tree.
The gun can't be unfired. The drink
        stays swallowed. And the stupid,
bloated rhetoric that passes for patriotism
        can't be unsaid. Wishing the past undone
is not remembrance, but regret.
        Memory can become an amnesia,
a blind going forward, crafted to deny
        we could do anything differently
or fashion any outcome better
        than these stay bullets, these fallen
trees and flags lowered in acts of mourning
        we remain too unconscious to name.

ELECTRICITY: A REQUIEM

In the commencing: a song. Fire below earth's rim, a brand
        of coronation.
Thunder-rattled. Throat-stuck. What sparked blue across
        the half-built lobes
of the first man to register lightning breaking into veins
        across a dark backdrop
of sky, promise of how thin creation could be, everything breaking
        in an instant of fire and noise.

§

How could fire not be confused with God the first time
        it was delivered,
sudden heat, quick opening in the dark? Wanderers learned how
        to carry fire with them,
not sensing yet that its warmth, its gift of vision would lure us
        into building hearths
to cast our bodies beside?
                            Now, pre-dawn. First blot
        of crimson cloudy
behind trees, before rising, defining roofs, dew-beaded
        and cold hoods of cars.
The porch light that burned all night, that was, an hour ago,
        a beacon
pales now in the crooked arm of the valley, as houses stew
        with lamp-light, shaking away
sticky webs of sleep, dreams not done having their say.

§

Mississippi and Louisiana, searching for quicker, less expensive ways
        to kill prisoners, elected
to buy electric chairs that could be taken around the state rather than
house
        the soon-to-be-dead in Parchman

or Angola. Crowds would come to watch the chair unloaded. The executioner
        would hire an electrician
to wire up the chair. In some towns there were concerts and picnics.
        Church bells would toll

as the hour approached. When the condemned man was hooded and strapped in,
        When a stranger's hands took the switch.
generators, unaccustomed to such loads, groaned. Every light in town dimmed,
        then burned bright and hot again.

§

Figure the odds. Your chance of being hit by lightning is the same as your chance
        of winning the lottery.
But you buy tickets for the lottery. Your ticket for lightning is your existence
        on earth.
                A century ago, an enterprising arborist laid bricks
        in the jagged rift
lightning tore in the great elm outside my grandmother's bedroom window.
        I know nothing
of what it takes to save trees.
                        I know or once knew how to run pipe,
        pull wire for the sockets
and fixtures that bring the lightning song of electricity into our homes.
I still
        know what to fear.

And the gamble. One man is killed by a charge that hardly tingles

another.
       A drill bucks
and a heart sparks to its stop. Another heart courses on even after three
thousand volts
       blast through it, burn hair
                           to a dry waste, melt shoes to the
floor.

§

The name of the writer changed from year to year, but not the story.
       It was always
a writer from the south, disemboweled by whiskey, crawling
       the yellow line

of the state highway through town. Arrested, processed, he made
       his one phone call
to Miller—it was always Miller who was called when
       the story was told—

to say he needed to get out of jail before he was executed in
       the town's electric chair.
Attempting reason, Miller was say, "Well, (you fill in the blank here),
       this is a small town

and I don't believe we have an electric chair."
                           "Miller,"
       the distressed writer would say,
"Miller, it's a very small electric chair."

§

When the executioner and electrician got too drunk to correctly wire
        Louisiana's traveling chair
"Gruesome Gertie" and kill Willie Morris, he screamed until
        the current choked off.
Those collected to watch him die went home. Later Willie Morris said
        death tasted like peanut butter,
that it was as shiny as sparks the sun shook from a rooster's tail.
        A year and nine days later,
two sober electricians ran the chains and spurs of electricity through
        Willie Morris's body
and sent him across the river, beyond the reach
        prayer and testimony.

§

We were thirteen. The boy on the bike was ten. We knew him
        the way boys in little towns,
in neighborhoods, know each other. So when the truck hit him, we
knew
        it might have been

any one of our bodies launched into another life, saddled in
        a wheelchair, body gone
thin and pressure-sored. And no one wondered how a boy who could
        barely move his arms

pulled a plugged-in radio into his bathwater, his life strangled
        by the blue flower of electricity
blooming fire in that water, shocking his spent body with power
        pulled from the buck and hum

of turbines, the growl of water dammed for acres, the greased
        revolutions of machines sliding

their power down the branched cables into the vein-works of wires,
        the tiny mouths of outlets,

the brain-fine filaments of bulbs that extend our vision deep
        beyond the hours marked
for sleep so windows glow unblinking, translucent as tears on the faces
        of those left to mourn when

the current was shut dead and men and women turned from
        the mid-day execution
to walk home for quiet copulations in shade-cooled houses,
        then a nap as afternoon's shadows stretched into shroud.

FROM *SLEEPING THROUGH THE GRAVEYARD SHIFT*

(2020)

PHENOMENOLOGY

In Madrid, he bought a pack of Gauloises, spoke a long time
to a woman buying fruit before walking out,
                                        his white suit
shining, his steps precise as a dancer's. In San Francisco
he shuffled a brief buck and wing before a sidewalk band.
Somewhere in Mexico, he received communion, then stopped a vendor
and bought shots of the homemade tequila that made
an encumbrance of the body.
                        Outside Fatima,
the shepherd children who saw the Virgin Mary in 1916
felt the sun slow its immolations long enough
to see a heart glowing clear as the center of a fire
and they heard
                Mary speak from the deep blank of sky,
                                                making
the children helpless vessels, their old lives spilled,
and all before them blocked by what they'd seen.
It's uncertain
                what happens when the body shrugs and dies
though it seems some stay to dance in white clothes
and others vanish like furniture
abandoned on the curb.
                        While the battlefields
of Europe split with fire, Mary told three frightened,
illiterate children that if her words were heeded,
peace would follow.
                        The man seen on the streets
of half a dozen cities, sported a white linen suit
twirling a gold headed cane,
                        while the body
that had borne him for almost eighty years rested, for once,
still as a stone.
                        And no one reported any words from him
though he flickered through a handful of afternoons,
the smoke of his last cigarette hovering
in all the last places he was seen.

A CHINESE POET CONTEMPLATES HIS JOURNEY

The moon tonight means less than the sliver
          of fingernail I trimmed while I waited

for my wine. To the left of me, wars
          and the stories of wars. From the right,

mythologies and dust. I wish there was
              someone to play music. I would pay them

for a song that would help erase all
          that is looming and distant. I wish

I did understand one word I hear
          spoken around me. This purple wine,

this bench where I sit, the sun whose warmth
          lingers, like me, long into evening,

these are all things I hold dear tonight.
          Behind me, a grave. Before me,

another. Soon leaves will whirl
          and die, yellow tongues crisping brown.

The stark penmanship of trees will be written
          against a sky swept bare

as the stones I climbed to the school
          where I learned poems and numbers,

where I learned some roads led
          to the borders of this kingdom,

and some traveled beyond.

LOVE IN VAIN

For DB

If we could make mixtapes for those departed
into the silence of the afterlife, there would never be

room enough to include all the music necessary,
and I'd be left to curse the song I'd deprived

some friend or loved one from hearing throughout
the long aftermath. Tonight I'm thinking of "Love In Vain,"

the one song by Robert Johnson I can't find
mentioned in your book of the blues. For half an hour,

I've switched between the dust-born noise
of Robert Johnson's version and the rendition offered by

The Rolling Stones on *Get Your Ya-Yas Out.* More time
has passed since the Madison Square recording

than between Johnson's first recording and the Stones' cover.
Johnson sounds weary as a bad year as he watches

his baby leave on the train for Lethe or some shade-tangled
branch of the underworld. Two lights, one red, one blue,

burn from the back of that vanishing train, a glow
to turn all desire to ash. The electric slide drawl

of Mick Taylor's guitar, Mick Jagger's fatback enunciations
that never quite erase London make the woman metaphor

for the desire of these men to tune and chord the black dirt,
the hangman's moon, all the sweet voodoo of the blues.

The Stones' baby, though, is not bound for hell, but London,
Manchester, Brawley, somewhere time-locked and sensible,
unlike Johnson's lover, whose fate lingers between the drawn-out
notes the guitar can reach, the crackle of dust like time unfolding.

I wish those lights, red and blue, had been enough to vanish
the anger that silenced correspondence between us

during your last months, when it was still possible
for you to hear those songs and remake them in the alchemy

of your poems. I don't believe any love is wrong, even
the ones that hurt us empty, that makes us moan

like a piece of metal slurring down the neck
of a guitar. I don't believe there is any song

that is not a yearning for something else. We are
creatures made restless with desire, forever riding away

or waving farewell, always believing
a stranger will descend from the dark platform,

take our tired arms, ask our names, convince us
that once, at least, love will not be in vain.

GHOST CRABS

Because the afterlife bears mystery
this dirt will not sustain, we learn
a new name for these armored crawlers
with their claws and briny scowls.
My daughter and her friend scrape
along the lacy surf line with a bucket
and small shovel, searching for
those burrowing nocturnals. They laugh
into wind that blows the sound away.
Tomorrow my daughter will be twelve.
Tonight she is content searching for
sand crabs—now ghost crabs--, beings
content to exist without us. In a few years
the joyous hazards of night
will arrive in dark cars, chrome
gleaming like blades, in the insincere
handshakes of boys I will never quite like
or trust, in all the temptations
I would take on for her if I could.
But she must dig into that dark sand
with her new hands, see for herself
the small, fierce things of night.
But that is a wave that has yet to break.
Tonight I'm pleased to peer into
her bucket, her cupped hands and see
the small, untamed life she holds.

DARK HISTORY

The sky, we praise always. The bones, never.
The plains and deep mountains sketched glories
we were told to worship. Never the crow.
Never the trickster beast. The eagle would
be our talisman. All written for us.
We could ignore the death songs bodies must
give in tribute to our circle of flesh.
The dirt, the grass, all earth was ours to take.
This was the myth that seasoned us. Rivers,
trees, coal would be infinite forever.
We could laugh at those who thought such things holy.
Whatever we restored would be reborn
as we secretly thought we would be.
Possibility would remain endless
for hands made to receive and shape the sky.

THE WAX CYLINDER: WHITMAN READING

No human voice could hold in such black clay, even allowing for the passage of time, the breath-shortened hills and gravel-floored valleys of the human voice needled into soft wax and saved. What you hear is the dust-crackle and white noise hiss, the span of years collapsing between our vigil here and Whitman, a quilt over his lap, a cat rolling in the parallelograms of light slanting through the windows while Whitman reads or recites "America" into the unnamed and unlistening void we call time.

When I was young, still too green to be one of the young men whose bathing Whitman celebrates, my sister and I cut cardboard discs from the backs of cereal boxes and played them on the boxy record player we shared, pretending we did not hear the static, the crunch of the needle grinding the shallow grooves, so we could hear The Archies or The Honey Bees singing through a moment when music seemed ready to take over the world.

However recording has changed, the sound of the voice and our fascination with capturing it has not changed. We love hearing what is said or sung, whether it is carved like a hieroglyph into wax or pressed into a scrap of memory deep in the wiring of a computer, where Whitman's voice is one click of information, poor vessel for the going-away words of a man who believed language could unite or at least name all the breaking apart fragments of a universe still beautiful in its mystery.

HARD LUCK: A REQUIEM FOR JERRY QUARRY

1.

First, the fist. The flat-knuckled hand, work scarred, lettered with
        India ink and a sewing needle, a letter on each finger

so his fists spelled *Hard Luck,* mantra for the low punches
        and cheap shots life deal out. The busted straight,

the dice that come up snake eyes, bad jobs, aching knees. Layoffs.
        All the small rages channeled into teaching his sons

to set their feet and throw a punch. Balance.
        The blow coming through the body , the next hit

coming from another angle, grinding his opponent's will
        into the sand no sweeping could clean from a plank floor.

"There's no quit in a Quarry," the old man reminds them
        until they believe it, breathe it, carry it

into rings all over the world, saving their fiercest fighting
        for one another, their sparring sessions stopping

all activity in the gym giving each other scars they carry under
        hard lights where they bleed and prove the old man right.

2.

My last vision of him, in the unyielding glare of a camera,
        as he shuffled, spoke in the broken syllables

of a man who has survived something horrible he can't recall,
        unwound the videos I've spent hours watching:

Jerry Quarry stalking the ring, never backing up, waiting
        for his opponent to make a mistake, patient

even when Ali or Frazier beats him to the punch,
        draws blood and slips the counterpunch.

In one video, the worn film stock overexposed and stained by light,
        the shot flickers as though time is sanding

the two fighters into chimeras, names released from bodies
        to become pure legend, like the unfilmed fighters

of centuries gone: John L. Sullivan, Peter Jackson.
        Quarry comes through wavering light, waiting until

one of his body hooks bends the other boxer. Then
        his hands fly like a drummer's, beating

the savage melody that is soundtrack to man's oldest sport.

3.

Too slow for games that required speed, too weak
        to supply power, I was left to prove my worth

in the improvisations of after school fights. Enough of those
        and you gain a little prowess, learn that pain

and blood end but end nothing. I knew that when I walked
        into the damp basement, its air curdled with sweat

and dead cigarette smoke of the old men who watched us
        flail each other and spit or grumbled directions

we couldn't hear or follow. Blood wouldn't end
        the sparring, but tears would.

The first night I was fed to someone older and meaner,
        whose job it was to make sure I didn't come back.

But Jerry Quarry's endless stamina has marked me,
        so I came back and spent the next few weeks

sparring with a kid more or less my size two or three
        nights a week. Neither of us inflicted or sustained

much damage, but we kept on, understanding
        the one who didn't come back first was the loser.

Some nights, leaving, I read the clippings in a glass case,
        aged tobacco-brown, brittle with age, triumphs of boys

better than we were, better than we could ever be.
        Next to one clipping, the obituary of a boy in uniform.

4.

Jerry Quarry was the single fighter to say yes when
        Muhammed Ali returned from suspension and needed

someone to fight. Since part of America had always wished for
        a great white hope in the ring and longed especially

for one to take out a draft dodger from the Nation of Islam,
        a red-headed hooking machine with Irish blood was made

to order. The fight was in Atlanta, an hour from us, but
        my dad stopped giving a rat's ass about boxing

before I was born. By then I'd given up sparring in the basement.
        If I wanted a fight, they were easy to find, but I'd been hit

and hit back enough to know that respect purchased by
trading fists is not respect, and winning fights has nothing

to do with justice. Even though I suspected Ali got a raw deal
    and Vietnam was no place to die, I pulled for Quarry

out of habit or respect. Who knows? The fight went the way
    of many of Quarry's fights in the 70s—he took

too many punches, began to bleed, and the fight was called.
    "He always cut too easy," Joe Frazier said years later.

5.

Hard luck. A phrase used to explain and excuse
    so much of Quarry's career. The words tattooed

across the old man's knuckles, the hairline split
    of scar tissue over one eye, then the other.

The first letters I ever saw tattooed on a hand
    were on a boy who appeared in eighth grade,

just back from training school, he told us. One hand, still
    a boy's soft fist, was lettered *Love*, the other *Hate*.

By the time I figured out training school was prison
    for those too young for prison, he was gone

though I'd see him walking here or there
    over the next couple of years, wasting time before

he vanished like he was never there at all,
    the way those letters faded into the dirt

of the body, the words little scars to mark
    the boy who once lived in that body.

6.
    For Jack Butler

The photograph was taped over my bed for so long
    I might have stopped seeing it: a page from *Sports Illustrated*,

Quarry fighting Jimmy Ellis. Quarry was taking a punch,
    his face twisted by the impact, his gloved fist lifted

to strike. He would lose this fight, his first shot
    at the heavyweight title. That picture stayed,

a flash of color like the picture I saved of Jimi Hendrix
    burning his guitar, those two photos bright planets

in a universe of black and white photographs of bands
    scowling from doorways, cemeteries, city streets,

a collection of glooms. Maybe that photograph taught me
    to love the ones who keep coming, whose art

is perserverance: the graveyard waitress, the hot tar roofer,
    the pitcher who takes the mound after being knocked out

of his last three games, the writer finishing his sixth
    unpublished novel, the band grinding through one more

rendition of a song popuar in 1978, the concrete finisher,
    anyone willing to bear the scars of a day's demands.
7.

I hadn't made an angry fist in a decade
    when I saw Jerry Quarry on TV, stooping

as he walked, his words a stumbling slur. He needed help
        to get dressed, to eat, as each blow he'd taken
echoed again, reclaiming a little more of what it took.
        Twenty years after what should have been his last fight—

he kept sneaking back to the ring like a man unwilling
        to let an old lover go—he was a palsied vessel,

lifting his fists again for the cameras.
        No words were lettered there, but in their rising

the old man said again, "There's no quit
        in a Quarry," a motto engraved in his son's flesh

deeper than any ink, any blow could ever reach.

FROM *THE BEASTS THAT VANISH*

(2021)

THE CONVERSIONS OF THE BODY

Neither red-faced coaches or
willow-wristed counselors,
too young for their beards, too anxious
in their desire to reach us,
could explain how we change
as we fall into life,
how we transform into bodies
shaped for the journey ahead.

Uncertain of constellations
spinning in the gut, the assemblies
of stars, the lifetimes required
for a spaceship to reach
the far suburbs of the universe,
I held my questions. The body
was both stranger and universe
and the church of flesh was all

I would believe in.
I heard stories of quicksilver
conversions, bodies trembled
in white-hot ecstasy at
the very lip of heaven. But
I never witnessed it once. A friend
who rolled his truck and walked away
without spilling his beer decided

to stop driving. Not the expected
conversion, but all he had
just then. He died quiet as breath,
sipping tea, reading e-mail,
his essence slipping into

the inconsistencies of the universe.
It's that essence ministers call for,
the same essence I inhaled
in the white noise of my knee
giving way to a careless blocker.
I vanished inside my breath.
The longer the pain held,
the longer I held the smoky center
of my being, the wounds

I would need to go forward. Say
we enter this borderless field
as energy and leave the same way,
our bodies and the lives they inhabit
vanishing into the shapeless
vowels of our final breath.

THE BOOK OF FORGETTING

By now she's tired of stories
      spotlighting her early deeds,
actions too endearing to be
      plotted, or the years before
she came, blanks of time distant
      as fires in the granite hills

west of us. Last week, a downturn
      in the atmosphere brought smoke
drifting raw currents only made
      visible by smoke's motion.
It trespassed flatland streets and yards.
      At bedtime, I whispered

her away from apocalypse
      and bad dreams, promised
clear skies, knowing my blood
      would pace sentry for hours
after neighbor lights went dead
      and the shrouded moon

took its perch in the sky.
      I know there is a book, more
than one, where the names
      of dead towns and their citizens
line the white pages neat
      as grave plots. We see

our place in that book once
      when we are born, once more
when we die. So I can't say
      the fate of anyone, of those
facing the flames, whether
      they weep or pray or howl

a fiddler's laugh. That's why
      I tell my daughter stories
we both know the ending of,
      so we can forget what truth
lies inside a book
      neither of us will read.

THE JESUS YEAR

What in this school yard, where the power saw whine
of kid noise splits open an afternoon gone electric
and rank with spring, reminds me

you would be almost 33 today? If you were ever born.
The Jesus year, my friends and I called it, as we saw it
rise before us, the careening of our twenties truly finished,

the near-calms of marriages and jobs that might last,
the notion of children, descending. And left behind,
the early wreckage. Including you. You and all the others

who arrived as fear and complication. Selfish, some say,
and I would not argue. Murder, others claim,
and I will leave them to what they think. We were

poor and mad and scared and young, to quote Jack Butler.
The drugs didn't help. Or the anger ignited, not drowned,
by endless cans of Budweiser. There is more to say,

but I am not the one to say it. Back then I said
We'll do what you want. It's your choice. Knowing exactly
what the choice would be. Unable to imagine it being different.

Kid, you would not have had a chance. In that time, that place,
the only choice would be the one we made. It isn't often
the past resurrects so violently, tearing at errors I'd already excused.

And you, nameless, genderless, never more than
a shadow trying to pass its dark palm over our lives, arrive
on the cusp of your Jesus year, one more ghost

of my past visiting me in this life I could not conceive
thirty three years ago, life where I often feel like a trespasser,
where I know part of my luck was in letting go of you.

THE BEASTS THAT VANISH

For Daniel Corrie

It was at one of those carnivals
        worked into extinction now, where

I saw the sign for a bear that would wrestle
        all comers, with a hundred dollar bill

for the one who lasted three minutes.
        My father pulled me past that tent

the way, ten years later, I saw parents steer
        their kids past the barker bidding

the men on the midway to come in and see
        the dancers. Behind him strippers

too young to know better or too tired to care
        crossed the little cat walk in front

of his tent. Those carnivals are memory now,
        hibernating in broken trailers and stories

of things that have turned into time's fossils.
        I wanted to see my father wrestle the bear, claim

the hundred dollars. I wanted to see the geek
        eat a live chicken. I believed the drawing of the bear,

its four inch fangs, claws like a fist
        filled with knives, rearing like a heavyweight

set to bench press the continent. I turned
        from the strippers' tent to walk

the midway, that trickster's alley
        whose one currency is illusion.

§

A late night documentary about Bigfoot asks
        if the creature is our collective invention

or a cousin lost on an evolutionary shelf. Each video
        dissolves into grainy light after

a few seconds or is taken from too great a distance
        to say what creatures we are watching.

Even the narrators of some videos express doubt
        about the shy creatures they've shot. More than once,

I've considered what it would take to vanish
        into the wide-set maw of this country.

And some have shrugged off the past, dressed themselves
        in a new identity. It can become habit:

a community college president left Maryland
        and surfaced a few years later

in an El Paso bar. Discovered, he went back
        to teaching until the itch returned

and he vanished again, crossing a line
        from curiosity into myth, a creature

no one could explain or catch.

§

There are night paths we feel but can't follow
        with our eyes, where each step becomes

a hazard, deliberation over whether a step
       or snare awaits, a steel trap set for

some predator, perhaps the beast
       you sense moving parallel and unseen

with you. In such dark, I could be
       anything, but not the animal

who knows the unfamiliar well enough
       to find a set of footprints and follow it

along the ridge time has cut, down
       into a past capable of birthing

creatures wise enough to vanish
       at our approach. They know

the narrow crevices that keep them safe
       until they decide to walk forward

within the shaking sights of man.

§

The bear my father and I finally saw
       did not wrestle, but sat

on a flat trailer, one leg shackled,
       tethered by iron links theatrical

in their size. Around the cuff I saw
       flesh rubbed raw, fur matted

and worn away. The bear was muzzled
    though he seemed more apt

to lick a hand than bite it. For the price
    of a chocolate Yoo Hoo you could watch

the bear take the bottle between two paws
    and swallow, his single trick.

A child in the fog-belted mountains of Tennessee,
    his head stuffed with myths

of Davy Crockett and trappers, could ignore
    the slow rain, the butt-heavy slump

of the bear. Somewhere under stars wiped
    clear of prophecy, a bear and her cubs

prowled unleavened dark. A hunter perched
    in a tree, half-slumbering

toward first light. And when that bear sat straight,
    a growl low in his prehistoric throat,

I was glad for the muzzle, the links
    that held him. Glad for the distance

of rumored creatures who walk their trackless path
    through the heart of time, trailing a scent

that kindles growls from those able to see.

§

In a few million years, the beings
      we will become, with their narrow fingers

and large heads, skin soft from rarely stepping
      into the half-toxic rays of sun,

may trade sightings of our kind, claim
      a few of us slipped through time unchanged

to walk as if earth had never changed and we could
      cast shadows wherever we please.

THE BIRD BORN OUT OF WEATHER

This sloppy mix, rain mingling with wet snow, dropped
all afternoon and into dark, sealing doors, silencing birds,

those little scraps of God or perhaps the disintegrating ego
of God. So in the morning, mud, no sound but water

dropping from limbs and eaves, a car down the street
revving to test the ice-skinned roads. By noon, roads will clear,

sun might even patch the ground. And a few sullen birds
will peck the soggy ground for what they can find.

But now, sleep dangles like the elusive silver bird
a boy from a story sees while out hunting one day

and chases until he has spent all his arrows, trying
to bring it down, until he is miles from any land

he knows, as far from sleep as the percussions of rain
and my own reckless brain have taken me. A story might

take years and this boy will be swept in a tumult of events
like a car spinning on black ice. He will travel for years

away from the valley of his birth, until a toss of fate
returns him to the place he started, a place still known,

but changed. The few who recall his name know him
as a tale to caution children from wandering too far,

not this stranger marked by travel and foreign battles
who throws a near-stranger's shadow over lanes settled

and made different over the years. And though he knows
five languages and a thousand names for God, he walks

to the edge of the settlement, listening again for the silver bird
whose song he followed into the life that became his own.

STORMS THAT MAKE THEIR OWN NAMES

for Kevin Santos

The crape myrtle's bark is peeling,
                          long brown strips
disposable as old wrapping paper. We are deep within
the chapter of summer that promises rain every day
but rarely delivers.
                          Hurricane season is taking shape
in the ocean, storms brewing a blend
of wind and tide.

                          §

A friend once wrote me a letter—in the pre-computer days
when letters and long distance calls were the only way
to stay in touch with anyone—
                          in which his architect's hand sketched
a diagram of how hurricanes swirl to life.
                                              The rest
of the letter was about a New Year's Eve that I missed,
which included a drunk visit to my ex-wife's house
and an all-night bar.
                          There was also a section, not related
to New Year's, about seeing Faron Young and John Hartford
playing a concert on a riverboat stage.
                                    I still find that letter,
folded in the pages of one book or another, always
a different book. The letter ended with a warning that
I could never be a scholar unless I read
every word Mark Twain ever wrote.

                          §

This is the season of snakes
                          taking siestas on back steps;
the air whines with bugs. My ankles jewel
with mosquito bites, little crests of dried blood.

I wipe my brow, say again
                    We need
to get in the car and drive though there is
no place of real refuge.
                    We could unfold fifteen maps
before we find weather cool enough to abide.
And once we were there, the only thing to do
would be to turn around and come back home.

§

My friend died a few years ago,
                              more than twenty years
after writing that letter to me. I barely recognized
the barbered man in his obituary. But the official record
never says
              what we know of friends: the dishes that began
with recipes and evolved into improvisations,
                                        the litany
of nearly-nameless bands he loved. The night he swept us
out the door like a storm still making a name for itself,
insisting
              we go on a post-midnight canoe ride.
It was going to rain, we said. There was work
the next day.
              "This will add twenty years
to your life," he insisted.

§

The weather channel displays three storms,
two deep in the Carribean, one lingering south of Florida,
only one worthy of a name yet.
                              I should go out
and rake up the crape myrtle's curved bark.

This fall, its flowers will fall
                     so their juices stain
the sidewalk, tiny hearts washed loose of color. Odds are—
a gambler's guess—that two of the storms will blow
into nothing. The third might
                     skirt land and vanish into
the great empty or make a hard turn inland.
It's always too soon to tell.

§

There are weathers we have no refuge from.
                     We all carry
what will not be escaped. Sentences brash
as a steamboat whistle announce us. An untasted spice
sinks through layers of stew.
                     And one wide-awake soul
sees the moon and calls, "Let's add twenty"
to companions who push into moon-stroked waters
where those years are waiting.

PLAYLIST FOR A PHOTOGRAPH OF A RECORD BURNING

August 16, 1966

Only one boy looks full on
at the camera, his glare
scorching the glass lens, a challenge
to all the years to come.
The others stare, as they should,
raptured, into the barrel where
cardboard sleeves curl into ash,
leave the slower melt of vinyl.
A voice rises, calling
for more lighter fluid.

"Hot town, summer in the city,"
sings the radio and that heat
flowers and grows around those
closest to the barrel. This heat,
the ministers promise, is nothing
beside the fires of hell.
In the next years, some children
congregated here with fight in
or protest a war, hear Hendrix
beg to stand next to their fire,
to marry the wrong boy or girl
or the right one, and enter
their own individual hells.

First the records, then
the Beatles wigs and dolls,
the magazines, lunchboxes,
a plastic guitar branded
with their faces, smiles that held
even as the plastic stretched
and folded into ribbons
of toxic smoke. Then,
other records: The Animals,
Stones, Kinks, Sonny and Cher
all fuel for the righteous flame.

"Love is a burning thing,"
warns Johnny Cash, though
his records are not the ones
burning here. But someone
loved those records once,
enough to save dollars earned
babysitting or cutting grass,
enough to count them out
one by one to pay for what burns now
as though music could
be unheard. More lighter fluid

and the boy still stares,
transfixed in the eye
of the camera. A year
or two and he will hear
Arthur Brown sing, "I am
the god of hellfire," and wonder
if fire ever truly brought
salvation. Ahead of him,
just under the ashes, wait
moon landings, Nixon, Watergate,
glam rock, cocaine, Woodstock,
weapons of mass destruction,
disco, recession. He will learn
there is never enough fire.

SHOOTING POOL IN THE MENTAL HOSPITAL

Because memory is not the hovering bank shot that stops at the lip
   of the pocket and will not fall,
but the scatter of balls when the cue ball strikes, rolling
   hurried and random as roaches

scrabbling for cover in the just-lit kitchen of a greasy spoon, it's hard
   to say how we will read what lies there
once everything settles. The same memory that once struck mirth
   might flame in unexpected sorrow,

like walking again into the roadside chicken joint the night before
   Thanksgiving, 1977.
As soon as we walked in, a woman behind the counter began to scream
   that only queers and junkies

came in there and she was sick of it. She slammed into the back, the
door swinging
   in her wake and did not come back
though we could hear her yelling. A girl who wouldn't look at us
brought our chicken
   and we drove on,

wondering through full mouths what could have triggered the woman's
rage.
   The night before,
loaded on mescaline, it had taken us an hour to shoot one rack of balls
   from the table.

Everywhere we looked, impossible angles, endless sprawl of green
   possibility, the way
things should look when you are nineteen and unable to see beyond
   the next hour.

Our bad shooting and laughter began to draw dark looks from men
betting

money and pride, both
scarce in a town bitten in half by recession. And in two months
        I'd seen the owner and his son

beat customers so thoroughly ambulances were called. One of us
scratched
        the eight ball and we left
for a place quieter and darker, somewhere our madness could find a
corner
        and hide.

§

Years later, that same friend, by now a believer in the enlightenment
        suffering could bring,
was ambushed by a mix of blood and rogue neurons, and the world
        became his church,

all matter mantled in light that fell slow and rich, like a painting
        of light. Everywhere he looked
waited a new place to worship, a new soul to bless. Such ecstasy will not
        walk free long.

A few nights after I saw him praying on a church's front lawn,
        he was delivered
to a hospital and his pacing brain was slowed by drugs whose names
sounded
        like the gods of a faith

I'd never heard of before. When we were allowed to visit—this was
        a charter hospital,not a lockdown facility—my then-wife and I
drove out to see him. I tried
        not to taste the fear

I've always had of not being allowed to leave such places, the staff

and patients reading
what I would not say, shuttling me off to rooms where I would spend
days
        yelling for someone

to listen. But we sat a while in the cafeteria, then walked halls so calm
        I almost forgot
the misdirection bubbling under my heart. In the rec room, my friend
suggested
        we shoot pool

for a new car. The sticks were warped to parentheses, and the twelve
ball
        was missing, but we racked them up
while my wife played cards with a woman who spoke the whole time of
        her fear of devil-worshipers.

And there, in that place that housed the God-touched and the devil-
frightened
        I shot the best pool I ever have,
the madness of those rooms conspiring with my body to bring me some
touch
        of earthly if not divine grace.

§

There are no martyrs in pool halls. Or standing over boiling pits
        of grease in chicken joints.
Sooner or later, the cost of what you sign up for becomes clear.
        And neither rage nor madness helps.

And if you had looked into the room that day and saw two men
        shooting pool
for imagined stakes, could you have said which was believed to be mad
        and which could pass for sane?

STERN

The first poem I heard him read—this was
on Bill Moyers' TV show about poetry—was "The Dancing"
about a family's unplanned twirl of ecstasy in the last year
of World War II, the three of them, young Stern
and his parents, not so young but younger, I'd bet, than I am
writing this, all dancing, the father using hand and armpit
to squeeze out farting sounds, the three of them
safe from and irreducibly caught in the wheel
of history. From here, the cities of the 40's seem
like benevolent wildernesses that now exist only in myth
where men in loose clothes stroll the boulevards, wearing
hats and ties and women wear pencil skirts, everyone
smoking. Jazz rolled from some windows, symphonies
shrouded darker windows. Bars were filled with shadows,
free of TV screens. Doors stood open because no one had
air conditioning yet. I taught Stern's poem for a few semesters
until two students, who enrolled thinking it would be
the easy A it was before I began teaching there, demonstrated
their arm fart technique for the class. This was at a school
for rich fuckups, many simply waiting for the trust fund
to begin paying off like a slot machine. But from then,
a few emerged to love poems for at least a year. Still,
"The Dancing" never made the pirouette back into the rotation.
If you teach, you know the drill—you learn which pieces
will teach something and lean on those until they have
no more to tell you, then find a few more. Or maybe
you choose a book or two each year and stumble through,
never sure if you've said anything worth saying.
Thirty-two years of five classes a semester and I've learned
which lessons I can trust. And my taste runs counter
to my students who are raptured by waterfalls, fields
of green frosted by Wordsworth's daffodils
while I try to explain the blossoming joys of decay,
of alleys through poor neighborhoods, the acne
of rust on a car left abandoned on the highway.
I never punched a clock in a coal or steel mill or I would sing

a spot for them in the pantheon as well. And the pantheon,
that endless, mythical anthology, is where
we all hoped to be going when we sat in workshops,
then later in bars, basking in some small triumph or nursing
wounds we would forget. It was the fall I got divorced
when a new professor handed back my poems and suggested
I read Gerald Stern, advice I put aside with a lot of other
good suggestions. It was a few years later, after school
was done, that I heard Bill Moyers talk to Stern
and went looking for his books. I was landscaping
in the day and teaching composition at night. Somewhere
I learned that he had spent years in community colleges,
a fact that fills me with joy when there are papers
to grade and poems that want to be written. The first time
I saw Stern was at a writers' conference as he moved
slow as a planet amid a constellation of smaller poets.
Heavy with mirth and awe, his face might have belonged
to the deli owner who rings up your Reuben. Or
the ring watcher telling you that the middleweight who keeps
dropping his left will never move up the card. Better dressed,
he might have been the lawyer drafting the Talmudic passages
making it possible to leave your estate to your fat dog
and not the grandkids who never visit or call. I'm old enough
to have outlasted some of the world's fascination
with youth. I can tell the students in my class, the Botoxed
ladies where I buy groceries that little runs
as wild as an old man's heart. Those fires are the ones
I need to keep this pen moving across the page.
Tonight, somewhere north of me, I hope Stern is writing
a poem. When I saw him read a few years ago,
we talked about community colleges and he signed
his book "Your fellow slave," though it's been years
since he was slave to any job. I left the reading,
grateful for the angels of poetry the ones whocome
on half-sprained wings to bless all that rusts and ages,
who come to us when we are wild enough to dance.

PUMPKIN SPICE AND THE INFINITE HORIZON BLUES

Brown-shoed, seated in straight rows, we were taught
and believed the impossibility of measuring the horizon.

Today, waiting in line for coffee, the horizon seems as good
a goal as any, especially when a latte order goes

into greater detail than the directions Columbus had
when he cast off on what promised to be a new route

to the West Indies. Of course, he never got there. And customers want
no discoveries in their morning drinks. In front of me,

two women talk about the return of pumpkin spice as though
it was a ship returned after three years' absence, its hold filled

with spices enough to flavor endless meals, silks to clothe
a succession of queens and, most important, to make the captain

endlessly rich. What we knew of endlessness was the flat hour
before school ended, leaving us to navigate the slow walk home.

I don't recall when pumpkin spice bloomed into a flavor
that spread over late autumn like a cloud, but I know it was not

one of the spices Columbus hoped to fill the hold of his ship with.
Columbus never found the riches he thought should be his

by right of invasion, sat chained and coughing for six weeks
in a Spanish jail at the end of his New World adventure, even

his theory about the shape of the earth fallen into disrepute.
The narrow view of the horizon available as I walked home

or stared slow and wide out the window said
our boundaries were defined, a pencil slash along

the edge of a yardstick. Venture far enough from shore
and the horizon grows until it surrounds you, a tilting

indifference you notice gradually, then realize you must pursue
until the pursuit becomes like an obsession with riches, a piece

of music that demands to be heard over and over. In front of me,
a woman orders a soy latte, skinny, half-caf with extra foam

and a splash of something. Each year I drift a few knots further
from the shore where my students stand. I sip my plain coffee,

black, and recall that when I started teaching a joke about Nixon
fetched laughs. Now their brows furrow if I mention Dick Cheney.

The sooner they can silence my arcane concerns, the sooner
they can return to cell phones and pumpkin spiced coffee that turns

their eyes dewy with sugar. It takes a while to see how a journey can
slip off course and longer to understand that drifting off course is

the true purpose of journeys, especially when the horizon moves
so the distance between us is constant and as impossible

to measure as the weight of steam rising damp
from this cup and all the cups before it.

EINSTEIN'S VIOLIN

Music builds itself, somehow, on numbers,
                                    a house that rises
so naturally we forget it has architecture, a plan
that might be studied for years, but never mastered.
Years of practice and still the foundation might float
unanchored or the placement of fingers fail.
                                    The small improvisa-
tions
that make an adventure of melody might slide by unheard. You could
play for years without learning to recognize the swerve
into a chord that shifts the tune's field,
the way Einstein believed
                                    planets might alter the focus
of gravity. Physics, after all is built of numbers as well,
its long-limbed equations built to probe
the architectures of the universe.

Some know the bodies of instruments as well
                                    as those
who spend their energy charting the heavens, watching for
new eruptions among constellations they know like the names of
their children.
                      Last night, leaning against the stage, I wondered
if the guitar player saw the small brilliance of Venus, the infinite
measures encased in an instrument when he tipped his head back,
let his eyes roll shut and let his fingers stir a cauldron of notes,
that blossomed, then faded
                                    into white noise that swallowed
all that lay before it.

If the drummer or keyboard player
                                    missed a note,
time stumbled, then found its footing. Unlike gravity,
music is not shared equally.

There is no place I know
where gravity differs to any degree we can measure.
But it is possible to tell the good player from the not-so-good,
to read who is playing and who is phoning it in for the night.

For those who are scholars of nothing in particular,
one entertainment is watching those who know their business.
When one scientist's book makes its argument for
one construction of the universe
                                              while his friend
argues for another way of coercing the same arrangement
of space and time,
                         I find some joy in knowing
there is no final answer,
                                    the way two pianists might
make different tunes of "Stella by Starlight."

I've seen enough pictures of Einstein holding a violin
to wonder if anyone recorded
                                         his playing. A search
through the dustbins of the internet told me
there was a recording of Einstein playing
Mozart's Violin Sonata KV 378, but a little more reading
told me this recording was fake,
                                           Einstein's playing attributed
to Carl Flesch. Without anything to hear
and only the testimony of his wife and friends,
                                                          we are left
to wonder what constellations took shape while he played,
what new equations timed the age and velocity of those universes?

Did he conjure the humming between spheres that is
                                                                almost music?

He would come from his study, pick up the violin
or sit at the piano and play, his mind revolving
in the deep reaches of this universe or the next one.

I can look at a page of sheet music or math problems,
but read nothing,
                    but I know the sound of the music I love
when I hear it, even if its making remains as mysterious
as mathematics or the unreadable realms of stars.

Maybe all the universe is navigated
                                    with numbers,
measures of the incorporeal waves that govern
time and space,
                    commanding that we age one-half breath
at a time. So each clock tick is both
a tallying up and a subtraction.
                                    Even while your fingers
gain velocity over the keyboard, the instrument of the body
is pummeled by gravity, a pressure that remains
constant and uncounted.

We have all come awake
                    to a voice that stopped
just as our eyes opened, the secrets breathed away
the instant an eye registered light.
                                    Sometimes
in that hovering where the body has
no particular beginning or end,
                                    I'm struck by a line
ringing fire, and, for that moment, true as a chord.
                                                        Then
I must decide whether to find a notebook and write it down
or believe it linger through my single journey
of sleep.

Last time I did this I wrote, "Slow lunch.
Matches. Bring dolphins and worry," a constellation
I will never navigate.
                    I retreated to the window,
where I counted a few houses still lit,
burning their way to or from the eternal dawn
where Einstein crafts a slow melody,
the start of a day's mysterious universe.

ABOUT THE AUTHOR

Al Maginnes was born in Massachusetts and was raised in a number of states, mostly in the southeast. He has degrees from English and writing from East Carolina University and the University of Arkansas. His poems, reviews, and music criticism have appeared in journals and anthologies , and he is the author of thirteen collections of poetry. A former winner of a grant from the North Carolina Arts Council, he was a founding member of Liberty Circus, a music and spoken word collective dedicated to social justice. He has worked as a hammock weaver, an electrician's helper, a warehouseman, a surveyor, and, for thirty-two years, as an English professor. He lives with his family in Raleigh, North Carolina, where he works part time as a ride share driver when he is not reading or writing.

www.ingramcontent.com/pod-product-compliance
Lightning Source LLC
Chambersburg PA
CBHW030918090426
42737CB00007B/233

9 781952 485992